AI Economics

Growth, Organization, and Society in the Age of Intelligence

Author Jason Y. Liu

Reimagining the Future of Business in the Age of Artificial Intelligence

— Preface to the trilogy "AI Economics," "AI Management," and "AI Marketing"

This is an era profoundly transformed by AI. From the macro landscape to micro-level practice, from societal operations to individual lives, artificial intelligence is reshaping every industry and rule. For enterprises, this transformation is not a gradual improvement but a civilization-level leap that rebuilds business, organization, and growth paradigms from the ground up.

This leap brings enterprises unprecedented challenges and opportunities. How to turn the wave of change into a powerful engine for self-evolution is a question every entrepreneur and founder faces. Haier has defined 2025 as the "First Year of AI Applications," embracing AI comprehensively, across the entire workforce and all processes; "co-evolving with AI" has become a shared consensus among all employees. AI is evolving from a tool for reducing costs and increasing efficiency into a core capability driving business development, becoming the new genetic code of Haier's products and services, and on this basis propelling a comprehensive, end–to–end transformation and reconstruction of strategy, organization, R&D, manufacturing, and services.

No exploration of transformation can be separated from the collision with high–quality ideas. I have known Jason Liu for nearly thirty years. He has been deeply involved in hands–on practice within China's manufacturing and retail systems, while also pioneering cutting–edge AI applications in North American real estate marketing, giving him a unique perspective that spans Eastern and Western markets. This accumulation of "unity of knowledge and action" keeps his observations grounded in reality, far from empty talk. When he distilled his thinking into this "AI Trilogy," what I saw was an old friend's serious contemplation and proactive response to the questions of our era.

His trilogy builds a complete cognitive system: "AI Economics" unveils the inevitability of paradigm shifts and explains why traditional growth models have failed; "AI Management" addresses the core question of organizational survival and provides an architectural blueprint for future "human–machine symbiosis" organizations; "AI Marketing" systematically explains how to achieve sustainable growth in the intelligent age. The trilogy not only poses the question of "why," but also offers the "how." Its reflections on topics such as "super individuals," "agent networks," and "organizational restructuring" resonate with Haier's transformation, offering a valuable frame of reference for examining our own practice.

The best way to predict the future is to create it. As the dawn of AI illuminates the business world, we are not only witnesses but also creators of this transformation. Enterprises that are first to embrace AI, reshape their organizations, and innovate their models will gain an edge in the new wave of competition and become protagonists of the AI era; those that cling to tradition and remain complacent will be eliminated by the times.

Overall, this trilogy is a practical thinking framework distilled by Jason from China's real-world business experience, the systematic logic of Western business theory, and long-term observation of future technology trends, opening a window for readers into an intelligent civilization.

For entrepreneurs, individual founders, and young people who feel uncertain about the future, this is a fine gift. It not only provides tools and methods, but more importantly offers a cognitive model for re-understanding the self, organization, and value in the intelligent age.

The future has arrived; it is just unevenly distributed. In an era rewritten by AI, whether an enterprise can endure ultimately depends on whether its cognition can continue to evolve. I believe this is the most important value of this trilogy.

With this foreword, I recommend it to all entrepreneurs who are contemplating the future.

Chairman and CEO of Haier Group Zhou Yunjie

CONTENTS

Introduction

The Gateway to Intelligent Civilization—Costs, Paradigms, and the Future

0.1 The Core of Economics: The Game of Costs and Three Historical Leaps

All economic theory, at its root, revolves around "cost." Whether it is Adam Smith's division of labor or Coase's transaction costs, the essence is an inquiry into how to reduce a specific type of cost in order to achieve a leap in efficiency.

If we compress the past 300 years of human economic history into a single film, we will witness three decisive cost leaps. Each technological revolution was not a "plug-in" added to the existing economic system; rather, through the collapse of a core cost, it directly altered the operating logic of the entire economy:

The First Leap: The Collapse of Physical Costs (Steam Engine)

The essence was that, for the first time, humans were able to replace "physical labor" at scale. The steam engine, electricity, and the internal combustion engine made the physical costs of manufacturing and transportation unprecedentedly cheap. This gave rise to the modern factory, global trade, and a consumerist society.

The second leap: the collapse of information costs (the internet and digitalization)

The essence was to push the cost of information exchange close to zero. Computers and the mobile internet made copying, storing, and transmitting information no longer expensive. This gave rise to multinational companies, digital platforms, and social networks.

The third leap: the collapse of intelligence costs (artificial intelligence)

And in this AI revolution we are experiencing, its essence is the dramatic reduction of one of the most expensive costs in human history—"intelligence costs."

This time, AI is no longer an "update to the tech industry," but, for the first time, makes it possible to replicate human thinking, judgment, decision-making, and cognition at scale. Just as electricity allowed "power" to be infinitely replicated, AI allows "intelligence" to be infinitely replicated.

0.2 Intelligence costs: humanity's final cost barrier and a new factor of production

Intelligence costs can be broken down into two core components, and changes in these two parts make

AI a brand-new factor of production:

1. Cognition Cost (Cognition Cost): the cost of "thinking"

The costs of all mental labor, including learning knowledge, analyzing problems, making judgments, and making predictions.

Before AI emerged, high-quality "intelligence" was extremely scarce and expensive. It depended heavily on a small number of well-trained elite minds (such as doctors, lawyers, and engineers). Today, large language models (LLMs) are, in a discontinuous and nonlinear way, turning "intelligence" itself into a public utility that can be massively replicated, invoked instantly, and delivered at extremely low cost—just like electricity and tap water.

2. Action Cost: the cost of "execution"

Including the costs of turning the results of thinking into concrete actions and adjusting based on feedback. When intelligence becomes a cheap factor, classic economic models face breakdown.

Traditional economic models (such as the Solow model and growth accounting) mostly assume: labor and capital cannot be infinitely replicated, productivity exhibits diminishing marginal returns, and innovation depends on human accumulation. AI changes all three:

Non-rival capital: Traditional capital (machines, factories) wears out with use and becomes more expensive. But an AI model, once trained, can be deployed infinitely; the more complex the task, the more the AI can learn.

Increasing marginal returns: In traditional models, the larger the company, the higher the management costs. But AI can automatically manage processes and allocate tasks. In other words, the larger the enterprise, the higher the marginal returns of AI.

Innovation is automated: From writing papers and code to designing strategies, AI is lowering the threshold for innovation to the lowest point in history. Innovation cycles no longer depend on experts' inspiration, but on iterations in compute.

0.3 Paradigm shift: from "prediction machines" to "action machines" and the restructuring of labor

Professor Ajay Agrawal of the University of Toronto proposed a groundbreaking view in his book Prediction Machines: the essence of AI is a reduction in "prediction costs." This is a great insight, but it is only half right.

After 2023, as AI agent technology matured, AI has evolved from a passive "prediction machine" (giving you advice) into an active "action machine" (getting things done for you). It not only reduces cognitive costs but has also begun to significantly

lower action costs.

An AI agent can not only help you analyze "which stock is likely to rise" (cognition); it can also place orders automatically, monitor the market, and sell automatically once the target is reached (action). This "cognition + action" closed loop has completely restructured how the micro–world operates.

The labor market is being redefined: humans + agents

In the past, a job was made up of a "person": skills + experience + time = labor. In the future, a job will become a hybrid of a human + an AI agent. Real estate agent: no longer someone running themselves ragged, but "1 agent + 10 intelligent

agents" (responsible for writing ads, valuation, client follow–up, copywriting, and drafting contracts).

Lawyer: no longer a drudge combing through case files, but "1 person + 20 legal intelligent agents." The fundamental change in the labor market is: from "Who can do this task?" to "Who can leverage AI better to do this task?"

Corporate organization is being redefined: a bimodal distribution

As Ronald Coase once said, "Firms exist because market transaction costs are too high." AI has sharply reduced transaction, management, and coordination costs, leading to two extreme trends:

Trend A: Mega–sized enterprises (AI amplifies scale effects). The more compute, the stronger the intelligence; the more data, the stronger the monopoly.

Trend B: Super–micro enterprises (AI lowers the cost of starting a business). "1 person + 100

AI agents" super–individual companies are becoming a reality. Middle–management positions are eliminated, and small teams are extremely agile. Just like the "AI full–stack real estate company" you are building, which leverages AI to make a 1–person company operate like a 10–person company—a typical case.

0.4 Global economic landscape: Compute-rich countries vs compute-poor countries

AI not only transforms micro–level firms, but is also reshaping macro–level geopolitics. The world's economic landscape is no longer simply divided into "developed vs developing" or "West vs East," but instead features a new dimension:

Compute–rich countries vs compute–poor countries

The lower the cost of compute, the faster the innovation; the more data, the stronger the models. The more complete the AI infrastructure, the faster a nation grows. Future global competition will revolve around the following core areas:

Data sovereignty

Compute supply and chip manufacturing

AI population (i.e., the number of AI Agents) and automated industrial chains

AI is not just a tool for economic growth; it will become the core of national power. This means that wealth and growth will concentrate heavily in countries and regions that control computing power. Without intervention, this will lead to unprecedented global inequality.

0.5 The Core Framework of This Book

Centered on the core concept of "the collapse of intelligent costs," this book will systematically explore, from micro to macro levels, how it will reconstruct the underlying logic of the business world. The book will attempt to answer the following key questions:

When intelligence is limitless, how does the economy operate?

Which jobs will AI replace? How will wage structures change?

Will AI make industries more monopolized or more fragmented?

Will AI bring deflation or inflation? Will GDP grow explosively?

The structure of this book is as follows:

Micro level: We will examine how AI reshapes production functions, labor markets, firm boundaries, and management models.

Meso level: We will analyze how AI disrupts industry structures and gives rise to a "bimodal distribution" industrial landscape.

Macro level: We will examine the profound impact of AI on economic growth, inflation, global competition, and wealth distribution.

At the practical level: Finally, we will focus on concrete industry applications and enterprise-level strategies, and provide a clear action guide for every individual seeking to survive and thrive in the intelligent era.

For individuals, those who master AI will possess a tremendous advantage; for enterprises, managerial capability will be equivalent to the ability to orchestrate AI; for economics, models must be upgraded to explain future growth.

This is not merely a technological transformation; it is a civilization-level paradigm shift. Welcome to the threshold of the Intelligent Civilization.

Chapter 1

The Economic Essence of AI: The Nonlinear Decline of Intelligence Costs

Academic positioning of this chapter: From micro cost theory to the model of collapsing intelligence costs

Why did the Industrial Revolution make physical labor cheap, while AI will make intellectual labor cheap?

When the marginal cost of "thinking" approaches zero, do corporate moats still exist?

Before we discuss how AI will reconstruct business, we need to use microeconomics (Microeconomics) as a lens on costs and factors of production to understand the underlying gravity of this transformation.

I. The Cornerstones of Traditional Micro Theory

1. Scarcity (Scarcity): Economics is built on the premise that resources (such as high-intelligence labor) are scarce and expensive.

2. Increasing marginal cost: In traditional production, as output increases, the cost of acquiring additional resources usually rises (such as hiring more capable experts).

3. Depreciation: Traditional capital (machines) wears out with use

and declines in value.

II. Revisions to traditional assumptions (the rupture brought by AI)

Revision 1: Cost collapse. AI has caused a cliff–like drop in the marginal cost of "prediction" and "cognition," breaking the assumption of scarcity in high–skill labor.

Revision 2: Capital anti–entropy. Intelligent capital (models/data) exhibits an anti–entropy property of "getting stronger with use," overturning the law of depreciation.

Revision 3: Factor recombination. The core bottleneck in the production function has shifted from "human labor" to "computing power and data," reshaping the minimum viable architecture of the firm.

III. Forward-looking case: Morgan Stanley's reshaping of knowledge assets

To validate the "collapse of intelligent costs," we analyze the Wall Street giant Morgan Stanley (Morgan Stanley).

This institution, with 16,000 advisors, by connecting to OpenAI's GPT–4, instantly transformed hundreds of thousands of research reports and internal documents that had been lying dormant on its servers into "intelligent capital" available on demand. This is not merely a tool upgrade; it is a quintessential experiment in reducing the costly "cognition and retrieval costs" to zero.

1.0 Introduction: AI is not "another tool," but a "disruptor of cost structures."

If you only regard AI as just another "efficiency–boosting software" after Office and Photoshop, you will miss the full scope of this revolution.

All technological revolutions over the past few centuries share a common trait: they do not add a new industry; they reduce the cost of a core factor.

The Industrial Revolution reduced the cost of mechanical work. Electrification reduced the cost of energy transmission. The internet reduced the cost of information transfer.

The essence of AI is a violent revolution in the "intelligence cost structure." It does not merely make your P&L (profit and loss) statement look a bit better; it is rewriting your P&L statement.

1.1 Brief Introduction to the Traditional Economics Framework

(Theoretical Foundations of Traditional Economics)

The core task of economics is to explain how a society meets unlimited needs under limited resources. Whether Adam Smith or Keynes, all economic research begins with two most fundamental premises:

1. Resources are scarce (Scarcity): whether time, money, or land, they are never sufficient to satisfy everyone's desires.

2. Choices entail costs (Opportunity Cost): when you choose to do A, you necessarily give up the opportunity to do B; that is the opportunity cost.

Whether individuals, firms, or governments, all must make trade-offs among countless conflicting choices: How should time be allocated? How should budgets be used? How should talent be deployed? What economics explains is how humans make "optimal decisions" under constraints.

The following six core concepts form the foundation for understanding the modern business world.

(1) Cost and Efficiency: Marginal Analysis

The most important way of thinking in economics is the "marginal." Rational decision-makers do not look only at totals; they look at increments.

- A business owner does not think "Should I hire 100 people?" but rather "If I hire one more person, will the value they create exceed their wage?"
- Will the value created by hiring one more person exceed their wage?

A factory does not think "What is the total cost?" but rather "If I run the machines for 1 more hour, how much additional cost will that add?"

The comparison between marginal cost (MC) and marginal revenue (MR) is the core logic behind all decisions in economics. As long as MR > MC (marginal revenue exceeds marginal cost), the action is worth continuing. This logic has guided all business expansion over the past three centuries.

(2)Production, Costs, and Firm Organization (Production & Costs)

Traditional economics views firm production as a "black box" of inputs and outputs. The two most important input factors are:

- Labor (L): human time and skills.
- Capital (Capital, K): machines, factories, equipment, tools, etc.

Firms convert labor and capital into output through a "production function." The classic Cobb–Douglas production function takes the following form:

Here, A represents the level of technology (in traditional models, it is typically treated as an exogenous variable). In terms of cost structure, almost all traditional industries exhibit one characteristic: decreasing returns to scale.

Although at the initial stage, larger scale brings lower average costs (economies of scale), as organizations grow bloated, management costs rise sharply, leading to declining efficiency. This limits the boundless expansion of traditional firms.

(3)Price, Market, and Supply & Demand (Supply & Demand)

The most famous model in economics is the supply and demand

curve.

- The demand curve slopes downward to the right: the lower the price, the more people will buy.
- The supply curve slopes upward to the right: the higher the price, the more firms are willing to produce.

The intersection of the two is the market equilibrium price. This price is like an "invisible hand," automatically adjusting resource allocation so that the market is neither chronically short nor chronically oversupplied. In modern economies, whether it's the price of the iPhone, Uber fares, or housing prices in prime locations, they essentially follow this rule.

(4)Market Structure: Competition and Monopoly (Market Structure)

According to different degrees of competition, traditional economics divides markets into four basic structures:

- Perfect competition: countless small businesses with no pricing power (e.g., agricultural products).
- Monopolistic competition: products are differentiated, with some pricing power (e.g., restaurants, apparel).
- Oligopoly: a few giants dominate (e.g., aircraft manufacturing, telecommunications).
- Monopoly: a single seller (e.g., patented drugs, public utilities during certain periods). The formation of market structure is determined by entry barriers, fixed costs, and marginal costs. In the tra

ditional industrial era, industries with high fixed costs and low marginal costs (e.g., railways, electricity) tended to naturally form "natural monopolies."

(5)Information economics: incentives, symmetry, and decision costs

An important branch of economics called "information economics" reveals the real world beyond the perfect market:

- Information asymmetry: buyers are less knowledgeable than sellers, leading to adverse selection (e.g., the used–car market).
- Agency problem: the interests of the CEO (agent) may not align with those of the shareholders (principal).
- Transaction costs: to acquire information and monitor execution, firms must incur substantial managerial costs.

In the traditional world, information is expensive; obtaining it takes time, making predictions requires extensive human involvement, and decision–making relies heavily on experienced management hierarchies.

(6)The role of technology in traditional economics: exogenous (Exogenous)

This is the most crucial point and the biggest shock brought by AI. In classical growth theory (such as the Solow model), technology (A) has always been regarded as:

- Exogenous: like "a gift from the sky."
- A black box: we know it boosts productivity, but we don't know exactly how it arises.

Traditional economics cannot precisely explain the internal mechanism of "technological progress" and typically attributes it to random outcomes of scientific discovery. This is precisely the part that is most thoroughly rewritten in the AI era.

1.2 An overview of economic shifts in the AI era

(The Shift: What Has Changed?)

Artificial intelligence has not toppled the edifice of economics above, but it has modified the underlying "default parameters."

(1)Labor supply is no longer determined by population, but by compute

- Traditional: labor supply = population size × labor force

participation rate. Constrained by physiological limits(Humans need sleep).

- AI: Labor supply = Human labor + AI labor (Agents). As long as there is compute and electricity, digital labor can be replicated infinitely and work 24 hours a day. This is the biggest supply-side rupture in labor economics in a century.

(2)Technology is no longer exogenous, but an endogenous function

- Traditional view: Technology A is an uncontrollable black box.
- AI: Technological progress has become an engineerable function. A = f (ext{Compute} ,ext{Data} , ext{Models} , ext{Agents}). You can "stack" technological progress by purchasing compute, cleaning data, and training models. Technology has become a form of capital.

(3)Marginal costs approach zero, and industry structures move toward extremes

- Traditional view: Marginal costs decrease up to a point and then rise.
- AI: The inference cost of generating text, code, and images approaches zero. This causes digitally intensive industries to naturally display an extreme "head concentration (winner-takes-all) + long-tail prosperity (super individuals)" bifurcated structure, with the middle layer facing collapse.

(4)The matching mechanism shifts from "price" to "algorithm"

- Tradition: Supply and demand are matched through price signals.
- AI: Platform recommendation algorithms directly predict demand and create demand. Consumers' utility functions are no longer entirely endogenous; they are deeply shaped and guided by algorithms.

(5)Intelligent capital becomes a new form of capital

- Traditional: Capital = machines, factories (depreciate with use).

- AI: Capital = GPU, data, models (appreciate with use / counteract entropy increase).

(6)Enterprise boundaries are rewritten by agents

- Traditional: Coase's theorem holds that enterprise boundaries depend on the balance between transaction costs and management costs.
- AI: The five core costs of prediction, communication, supervision, coordination, and execution are all driven down by AI. Enterprises will evolve from a "pyramidal bureaucracy" to a "liquid network of agents."

1.3 In-depth case: Morgan Stanley

(Case Study: The Collapse of Knowledge Costs)

To ensure the above theories do not remain merely on paper, we introduce a Fortune 500-level end-to-end practical case. (Data sources: Morgan Stanley official releases / CNBC reports / OpenAI "AI in Enterprise" white paper)

I. Background: The giant's dilemma Morgan Stanley is one of the world's largest wealth management institutions, with over 16,000 financial advisors. Its core asset is "knowledge" — producing tens of thousands of research reports, market summaries, and client dossiers every day. But prior to AI deployment, these knowledge assets faced classic, high transaction costs:

- Access difficulty: internal documents are vast, with a utilization rate of only 20%.
- Slow retrieval: to prepare for a complex client meeting, advisors often need 1–2 days to find materials and synthesize viewpoints.
- Highly manual: review, cross-checking, and summarization all rely on human labor and cannot scale.

II. AI intervention: Reshaping the knowledge production system From 2023 to 2024, Morgan Stanley partnered with OpenAI to deeply embed GPT-4 Enterprise into its workflows, building the "AI@ Morgan Stanley" assistant:

- Full ingestion: hundreds of thousands of internal compliance documents were vectorized to form a unified "institutional brain."
- Empowering everyone: 16,000 advisors are all connected to the system.
- Automated production: AI automatically generates client meeting minutes, risk summaries, and draft investment recommendations, and automatically checks data consistency.

III. Quantitative results: The rewriting of the production function

- Efficiency leap: Information retrieval efficiency increased by 4 times.
- Asset revitalization: The utilization rate of internal documents surged from 20% to 80%. Dormant data has become active capital.
- Time released: Meeting preparation time was shortened from several days to a few hours.
- Role transformation: Advisors have shifted from tedious "information gatherers" to high–value "relationship and strategy experts."

IV. Economic insights Morgan Stanley's case clearly illustrates the core argument: the collapse of intelligent costs. When the marginal costs of "acquiring knowledge" and "generating judgments" shift from expensive human labor to inexpensive compute consumption, the firm's production function is rewritten. This is not merely a tool upgrade; it is a fundamental change in the nature of the factors of production.

1.4 The "discontinuous" decline of the intelligent cost curve: from prediction to decision

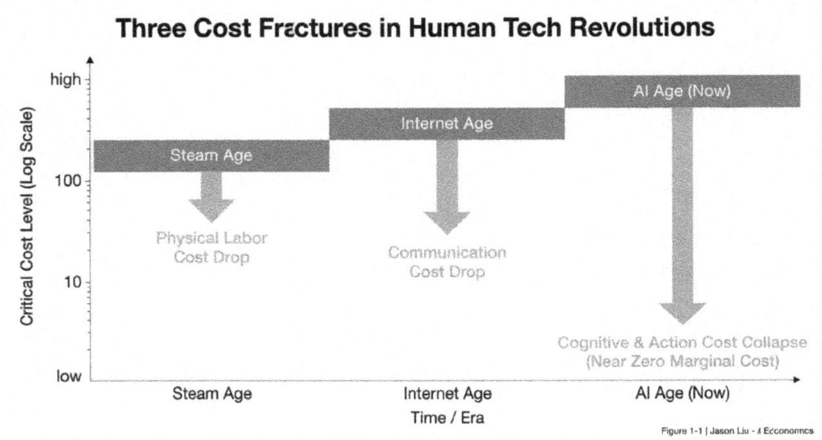

Economics is full of various smooth curves, but the decline in intelligent costs brought by AI is not a smooth curve; it is a "discontinuous" one. Within a very short period of time,

Drove down the cost of certain specific types of "intelligence" by several orders of magnitude. Core insight: the collapse of Prediction costs.

Canadian economist Ajay Agrawal proposed in Prediction Machines:

The core capability of AI is not thinking, but prediction.

In business, prediction is everywhere: banks predict risk, doctors predict conditions, executives predict strategy. In the past, these predictions were extremely expensive, relying on highly paid experts and seasoned managers.

But now, that cost has been crushed:

Case A (collapse of generation costs): In 2021, for a company to obtain a high–quality commercial image, it often had to hire a designer for hours of creation, with each image costing hundreds of dollars. By 2024, Canva, by integrating generative AI such as DALL–E, compressed this process to 30 seconds, and the fee plummeted from hundreds of dollars to just a few cents. AI is no longer merely "augmenting" existing steps; it has torn apart the originally smooth cost curve at the base layer, causing customer acquisition costs for content to collapse by a hundredfold for massive numbers of enterprise clients. [1][2]

Case B (collapse of decision–making costs): Contract risk predictions that used to require a legal adviser with 10 years of experience can now be initially screened by AI in 1 second, with a marginal cost close to zero.

This nonlinear cost collapse has made business models that were previously economically infeasible now viable. It has turned the once–scarce abilities of "prediction" and "judgment" into a general–purpose commodity, like electricity.

Business review: the "Before vs. After" of the collapse in cognition costs. "The decline in cognitive costs" is not an abstract academic concept; it has a highly impactful manifestation in real business

scenarios. Let's review a typical body of knowledge

Use an intensive workflow—investment analysts drafting industry research reports—to intuitively experience this change.

• Before AI: High cognitive load and time costs

Before 2022, a senior analyst would typically need at least 3 working days to complete an in–depth scan of the "embodied intelligent robotics market."

- Information gathering (40% of the time): Drowning in Google, Bloomberg Terminal, and industry databases, painfully sifting signal from noise.
- Reading and comprehension (30% of the time): Reading through dozens of hundred–page technical white papers; constrained by the bandwidth of the human brain, understanding complex

technology roadmaps consumes extremely high cognitive energy.

- Extraction and synthesis (30% of the time): Assembling fragmented information into a mental jigsaw and ultimately turning it into a structured PPT. This is the highest-order cost of structured thinking.
- After AI (2025): Agentic network collaboration and second-level delivery

Now, the same task has been reconfigured into an automated workflow. The analyst only needs to issue a single instruction, and a team composed of multiple specialized Agents begins collaborating:

- Search Agent: Instantly queries global data sources in parallel, scraping and cleaning 500 core documents.
- Reading Agent: "Reads through" documents at tens of thousands of words per minute, precisely extracting key technical metrics.
- Analyst Agent: Automatically builds an industry value-chain map, compares differences between technology roadmaps, and generates heatmaps.
- Writing Agent: generates clearly structured briefs.

The entire process was compressed from 3 days to 30 minutes, boosting efficiency by more than a hundredfold. More critically, analysts are freed from heavy "front-end cognitive labor" and can focus their energy on the strategic judgment of the final outcomes.

1.5 Intelligence Capital: a new production factor that counteracts entropy

Traditional capital (such as machinery and plants) depreciates and wears out with use—an entropy-increasing process. By contrast, an AI model, as a new form of "intelligence capital," exhibits a unique "anti-entropy" property, making it an unprecedented factor in the history of economics.

It has four unprecedented characteristics:

Non-rival: an AI model, once trained, can be used by countless people simultaneously. Unlike machinery, if you are using it, I cannot.

Learning-by-doing: as the model is used, it encounters more data, and through ongoing Fine-tuning and reinforcement learning (RLHF), its capabilities grow stronger and stronger. It "appreciates" in use rather than "depreciates."

Network effects: when an AI system (such as Tesla's FSD or Google Maps) gains more users, it collects more data and becomes more capable, thereby attracting even more users.

Infinitely replicable: inference costs approach zero. A shift in perspective from the viewpoint of mathematical models

To make the logic more rigorous, we can understand the firm's production function as follows:

Here, P is "forecasting and intelligence capability." In the past, P relied entirely on labor L (expensive human resources). Now P can be provided by AI, and the marginal cost $\partial C/\partial P\_AI \approx 0$. This means enterprises can expand their intelligence frontier without limit, without being constrained by the linear growth bottleneck of human resource management.

Consumer-grade network effects (Google Maps): The global route-planning capability of Google Maps does not remain static through fixed algorithms; rather, it learns every day from billions of users' real-time location, traffic, and behavioral data. With each additional user contributing traffic information, Maps' stock of intelligent capital grows. This network effect makes its route suggestions increasingly accurate, creating a positive feedback loop that continuously resists disorder (anti-entropy). [3][4]

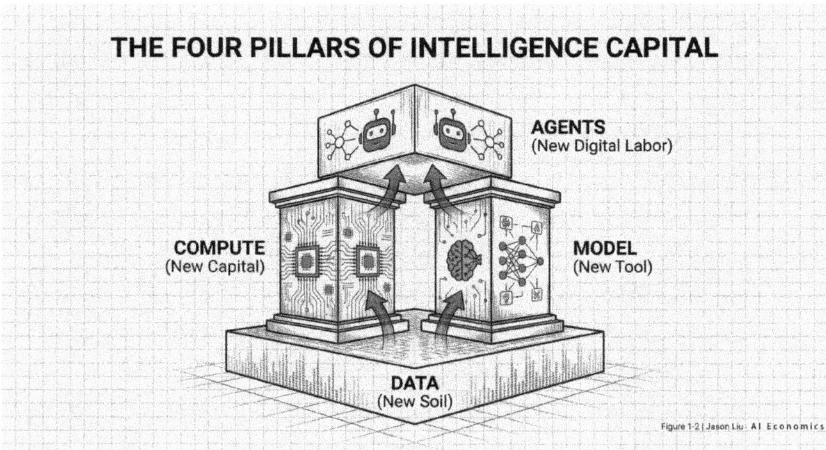

Figure 1-2 | Jason Liu · AI Economics

Enterprise–grade accretive effects (Salesforce): On the B2B side, after Salesforce introduced AI, it demonstrated the property of intelligent capital "getting smarter with use." As customer interaction histories accumulate, its models' prediction and recommendation capabilities continuously improve. This proves the fundamental difference between AI capital and traditional depreciating capital: it "appreciates through use." [1]

1.6 Scale effects of intelligence (Scaling Law) and three-layer evolution

Companies such as OpenAI have found that when large models surpass the tens of billions, hundreds of billions, and trillions of parameters, their capabilities undergo a "phase transition": evolving from basic dialogue to complex reasoning, code analysis, and multilingual collaboration.

This "emergence" is no longer confined to AI labs. Through a partnership between Microsoft and NVIDIA, by deploying ultra–large models on enterprise–grade cloud platforms, customers across vertical industries have leapt over the technology gap overnight. This scaling law is triggering monopolistic effects in the enterprise arena—only giants with the strongest compute infrastructure can provide such "emergent" intelligent services.[5][6][7]

This qualitative shift has driven a three-layer evolution of AI from tool to agent:

Layer One: Prediction. Able to assess probabilities and reduce analysis costs. Layer Two: Generation. Able to create text, images, and code, lowering the cost of content creation.

Layer Three: Action/Agent. This is the most critical leap. AI no longer just gives you advice; through Agents (intelligent agents) it executes directly—automated ordering, automated negotiation, automated workflow execution.

When AI enters the "action layer," it is no longer an auxiliary tool but a principal driver of productivity. This leads to AI's inherent tendency toward monopoly: only the largest models can exhibit the strongest action capabilities.

Ultimate form: Embodied intelligence and the zeroing of action costs

If large language models (LLMs) solve information processing in the virtual world, then Embodied AI is the key step for AI to enter the physical world and radically reduce "action costs."

According to the 2025 Embodied Intelligence Top Ten Observations Report, we are seeing general-purpose humanoid robots emerging from the lab. They are no longer automated robotic arms that only repeat a single motion, but intelligent entities capable of perceiving their environment, understanding complex instructions, and autonomously planning physical operation paths as intelligent entities.

When an AI can not only help you write a perfect business plan (zero marginal cognitive cost) but also control robots to make coffee, assemble parts, and even manage warehouses (action marginal costs approaching zero), the boundaries of human commercial activity will be completely rewritten. This signifies capital (machines) truly completing the comprehensive replacement of labor (the human body).

1.7 The marginal cost of intelligence approaches zero: the reconfiguration of enterprise organization

In the past, for each new client served, consulting firms had to assemble an expert team and expend costly hours, resulting in extremely high marginal costs.

Now, companies like OpenAI and Notion AI are "commoditizing" inference services through APIs and subscriptions: without adding any headcount, they can simultaneously provide thousands of businesses with "digital brain" services such as automated document analysis and strategy recommendations. AI drives the marginal cost of intelligent services toward zero, and this new model is rapidly becoming a disruptor in arenas like information services, document management, and programming. [2][1]

This not only ushers in a revolution in business models (subscriptions, API economy), but also more profoundly reconstructs the boundaries of the firm.

The failure and rewriting of the Coase theorem

Nobel laureate Coase proposed: firms exist because market transaction costs exceed internal coordination costs.

But AI drives internal coordination, communication, supervision, and forecasting costs to zero. This leads to a bipolar split in organizational forms:

Very large enterprises (AI amplifies scale effects): the more data, the stronger the intelligence, the deeper the monopoly (e.g., OpenAI, Nvidia).

Very small teams (AI reduces organizational needs): AI becomes "infinite middle management." A 10-person startup can, using Agents, accomplish the workload that used to take 100 people. Middle

Management—the essence of which is to transmit information and coordinate resources—will face the highest substitution risk.

1.8 Reality check: the "illusion" of intelligent capital and lessons from failure

While cheering the decline in intelligence costs, we must also beware of the trap of "technological determinism." History shows that possessing a new factor does not equate to possessing new productive power.

The Pioneer's Setback (IBM Watson): IBM Watson for Oncology once pushed medical AI at great expense, but was ultimately constrained by real-world limitations such as data heterogeneity and complex scenarios, failing to achieve its commercial expectations. This is a classic cautionary tale: without high-quality Data Quality, computing power alone cannot form intelligent capital. [8]

The Difficulty of Scaling (The Pilot Trap): A 2025 joint report by MIT and Fortune shows that over 90% of enterprise AI pilot projects ended in failure. These failures expose systemic challenges such as integration difficulty, slow deployment, and low ROI. [9][10]

It is precisely these failures that remind entrepreneurs to remain sober-minded: while AI's marginal cost approaches zero, the enterprise's Change Management Cost remains high.

Chapter Summary

The economic essence of AI is to leverage "anti-entropy" intelligent capital, achieve capability emergence through the "law of scale," and, via "zero marginal cost," massively commoditize "intelligence," once the scarcest resource.

This process is effecting a threefold substitution:

Prediction substituting for experience (no longer needing ten–year veterans).

Generation substituting for repetitive work (no longer needing junior illustrators/coders).

Agents substituting for managerial coordination (no longer needing a large middle layer).

This is irreversibly changing the basic cost–benefit structure of all industries.

Actionable Takeaways (Actionable Takeaways)

For entrepreneurs, investors, and individuals:

Conduct a "cognitive audit" and a "mid–management checkup":

Examine your company's largest cost item. If this spending goes to "repetitive cognitive work" or "middle–management coordination" (such as junior analysis, report writing, information routing, reviews), then this part of the business will be dramatically compressed by AI within the next 3 years. You must immediately look for alternatives, or you will be outcompeted by rivals who are not only cheaper but also faster.

Reevaluate your assets:

Your company's most valuable assets may no longer be plants or equipment, but those unique, high–quality proprietary datasets lying dormant on your servers. In the AI era, general–purpose models are like utilities, while your private data is the only fuel to train your own "intelligence capital."

Shift your mindset:

Stop asking "How much money can AI save me?" (this is stock thinking).

Start asking "When the costs of prediction and execution approach zero, what entirely new businesses—previously too expensive to attempt—can I create?" (this is incremental thinking).

For example: services that used to be too costly to deliver one–on–one at a premium level—can they now be enabled by AI ?

Innovations that we previously hesitated to pursue due to high trial-and-error costs—can we now simulate them 100 times with AI?

Chapter 2

AI Reshapes the Production Function: From Cobb–Douglas to "Intelligence Augmentation"

Academic positioning of this chapter: From the Exogenous Growth Model to intelligence–driven endogenous growth

Why can't merely piling up machines sustain a nation's long–term growth?

When "technological progress" is no longer a gift from God but computing power that can be purchased, where are the limits to growth?

Before we discuss how AI reshapes growth, we need the lens of macroeconomic growth theory to understand the underlying code of wealth creation in the industrial era.

I. The foundations of traditional growth theory

Diminishing Returns to Capital: In traditional industry, as the capital stock increases (for example, giving a worker a third computer), the additional output not only fails to rise but may actually decline. This means that relying solely on investment cannot sustain long–term growth.

Labor supply rigidity (Labor Supply Rigidity): Labor depends on the birth rate and physiological limits (people need sleep), which impose a natural physical ceiling and prevent unlimited expansion. Exogenous technology (ExogenousTechnology): In the classic Solow model,

Technology (TFP) is regarded as an inexplicable "residual," an uncontrollable external variable (luck).

II. Revisions to traditional assumptions (the rupture brought by AI)

Correction 1: Endogenizing technology. AI turns technological progress (A) into a function of compute, data, and algorithms. Growth is no longer about waiting for luck; it becomes a controllable engineering problem. Correction 2: Decoupling labor. Digital labor (Agents) breaks the constraints of population, achieving unlimited labor supply and 24-hour online availability.

Correction 3: Increasing returns to scale. Intelligent capital (models) follows Scaling Laws; the more you invest, the stronger the capabilities, breaking the traditional fate of growth convergence.

III. Forward-looking case: Microsoft's full-stack production function upgrade

To verify the "rewriting of the production function," we analyze Microsoft.

As the world's first super-enterprise to embrace AI across the full stack, Microsoft not only increased capital input (K, by purchasing massive amounts of GPUs), but also equipped every employee with Copilot (t expanding L), achieving a 55% improvement in GitHub code output efficiency. This is a perfect real-world example of growth driven by "endogenized technology."

2.0 Introduction: The production function—the "source code" of economic growth and the mystery of TFP

One of the core tasks of economics is to explain "Where does economic growth come from?"

The classic Cobb–Douglas production function Y = A K^\alpha L^{1–\alpha} is Understand the cornerstone of the modern economy. It tells us that output (Y) is jointly determined by the level of technology (A), capital input (K), and labor input (L).

In the traditional Solow model, capital accumulation cannot drive long–term growth (due to diminishing marginal returns); the only possible source of long–term growth is A (total factor productivity, TFP). But for a long time, A has been like a "black box," treated as an exogenous variable bestowed by God.

But in the AI era, every variable in this century–old formula is being redefined.

AI does not merely change parameters; it breaks two core assumptions of the traditional function:

- Diminishing marginal returns to capital and labor → reversed by AI's Scaling Law.
- The impossibility of unlimited expansion of labor and capital → broken by AI's unlimited replicability.

2.1 Traditional economics framework: the "source code" of growth

(The Code of Growth: Traditional Production Function)

In traditional economics, all explanations of "how the economy grows and how output is formed" rely on a core mathematical and logical framework—the production function. It is the lens through which economists observe the world.

(1)Production function: Economics' E=mc^2

The most classic and widely used production function is the Cobb–Douglas form:

This seemingly simple formula reveals three fundamental axioms of wealth creation in the industrial era:

1. Output (Y) depends on the quantities of capital (K) and labor (L) inputs.

2. The level of technology (A) determines the efficiency of converting inputs into output.

3. Technological improvement is the only force that drives the economy to break through resource bottlenecks.

Essentially, it tells us: national or corporate output = input scale × conversion efficiency.

(2) Capital (K): the core force driving industrialization

In the industrial era, capital is the explicit engine of growth: building factories, constructing highways, purchasing equipment. But capital has a fatal weakness: Diminishing Marginal Returns.

- Give a worker one computer, and efficiency rises dramatically;
- Give the same worker two computers, and the efficiency gain is limited;
- Give them three, and it may not help—in fact, it could become a burden. Therefore, simply "piling up capital" (such as endlessly building factories) cannot drive unlimited economic growth.

(3) Labor (L): a function of population

Traditional theory holds that labor supply is inelastic; it depends on:

Population size: there is strength in numbers.

Labor-force participation rate: how many people are willing to work.

Education level: it determines the quality of labor. Before AI appeared, the growth of the labor force was strictly constrained by physiological limits (people need rest) and demographic cycles (having children takes 20 years).

(4) Technology (A): a mysterious "black box"

In Nobel laureate Robert Solow's model, technology It is called Total Factor Productivity (TFP). It is the residual in the model that cannot be explained by capital and labor, and is therefore also known as the "Solow residual."

The conclusion of the Solow model is unsettling:

- Capital accumulation can only explain short-term growth.
- Only technological progress (an increase in A) can explain long-term growth.
- However, the model treats A as an "exogenous variable (Exogenous)."

This means that traditional economics acknowledges technology as paramount but cannot explain where technology comes from. It is like a "gift falling from the sky": economists can only observe it and cannot "produce" it within the model.

(5) Returns to scale and the limits of growth

Traditional production functions usually assume constant returns to scale (Constant Returns to Scale). If both capital and labor double, output roughly doubles as well. This implies that although large firms have advantages, they will not expand infinitely to swallow everything, because management costs and resource constraints create a "ceiling."

Summary of the traditional framework: The logic of economic growth in the industrial era is to jump-start with the demographic dividend (L) and capital investment (K), and ultimately rely on luck-like technological progress (A) to sustain. This is a pessimistic logic based on "scarcity" and "diminishing returns."

2.2 Overview of changes in the AI era: forcefully cracking the "black box of growth"

(The Rewrite: Why AI Changes the Equation)

AI does not render the traditional production function obsolete; it forces a version upgrade. It turns variables that were originally exogenous and uncontrollable into endogenous, engineerable ones.

(1) Redefining labor (L): from rigidity to infinite elasticity

- Traditional view: labor is constrained by population.
- AI: Labor = human labor + AI labor (Agents). AI can perform cognitive tasks (analysis, generation, reasoning) and can be infinitely replicated, operate 24 hours a day, with near-zero marginal costs. For the first time, the labor supply curve breaks free from the constraints of population cycles.

(2) Upgrading the form of capital (K): the rise of intelligent capital

- Traditional view: capital = machinery and plants (physical assets).
- AI: Capital now includes compute capital and data capital. GPU clusters, pre-trained models, and private data are not merely tools; they are "intelligent assets" that generate compounding effects.

(3) Endogenizing technology (A): Manufacturable growth is the greatest theoretical breakthrough. Technological progress is no longer a black box but becomes an object that can be "invested" in.

As long as you invest more compute, clean more data, and optimize better models, the technical level A will improve significantly. Growth becomes an engineering problem rather than a matter of luck.

(4) Marginal product: from diminishing to increasing (Scaling Laws) According to the Scaling Laws validated by organizations such as OpenAI, in AI models, as parameters, data, and compute increase, performance exhibits power-law growth. This means that in the core of the digital economy, returns to scale may be increasing. The larger the scale, the stronger the model; the stronger the model, the lower the cost; the lower the cost, the more concentrated the market.

(5) Energy coupling: a new physical constraint AI rebinds the production function to the physical world. Training a GPT-4-level model consumes enormous energy. Therefore, future growth functions must introduce Energy (E) as a hard constraint. Growth depends not only on intelligence, but also on the load of the power grid.

2.3 In-depth case: Microsoft × OpenAI

(Case Study: The First Upgrade of Production Function at Scale)

To prove that the rewriting of the production function is not merely a mathematical game, we introduce Microsoft's case. As the world's first super–enterprise to embrace AI across the full chain, Microsoft provides a perfect social experiment in the "AI production function." (Data sources: Microsoft Annual Report 2023/GitHub Research/CNBC)

I. Background: the bottleneck of cognitive productivity Microsoft is a typical "knowledge–intensive" enterprise, with tens of thousands of engineers, product managers, and lawyers. Under the traditional model, its production function is constrained by human cognitive bandwidth:

- Code output is limited: an excellent engineer can write only a limited number of lines of high–quality code per day.
- Communication costs are high: a massive organizational structure leads to slow information flow.
- Innovation depends on manpower: the development of new features relies entirely on stacking high–paid talent.

II. AI intervention: Full–chain upgrade of the production function. In 2023, Microsoft integrated the GPT–4 tech stack across the board, which is essentially a brute–force upgrade to its $Y=A\cdot K^\alpha\cdot L^\beta$.

- Copilot everywhere: Office, Windows, GitHub fully embedded AI.
- Expansion of L: Every employee is equipped with an AI copilot, equivalent to attaching a "digital twin" to each person, greatly expanding the effective labor supply.
- Qualitative transformation of K: Azure has become one of the world's largest AI compute infrastructures, shifting capital

expenditure (Capex) from traditional servers to an intelligent compute network.

III. Quantitative results: Nonlinear growth

- Explosive increase in development efficiency: GitHub Copilot boosts developers' coding speed by an average of 55% (GitHub official research). This means that without increasing the number of engineers (L unchanged), output (Y) increases by half again.
- Business flywheel: Azure AI services have become the fastest–growing business in Microsoft's history, generating over $10 billion in annualized revenue in a very short time.
- Document production revolution: According to Office Copilot user feedback, the time required for document generation and processing has been reduced by 80%.

IV. Economic insights Microsoft' s case answers the core question of this chapter: Why must the production function be rewritten? Because it proves that, in the AI era, capacity is no longer determined solely by "the quantity of labor," but by "the pace of expansion of the AI toolchain." Technology A is no longer something that falls from the sky; it is "forged" by Microsoft through tens of billions of dollars of investment in compute (K). This is a real–world example of endogenous growth.

2.4 The revolution of labor (L): the fusion of humans and "silicon-based labor"

AI has not simply "replaced" labor; rather, it has created an entirely new form of labor—"silicon–based labor" (Silicon–based Labor), namely AI agents (Agents). Their relationship with humans (carbon–based labor) is not a simple substitution, but a complex restructuring based on task models (TaskModel).

Acemoglu & Restrepo's task model perspective

If we break the production process down into a series of tasks (Tasks), the introduction of AI leads to three effects:

Task reallocation (Reallocation): Humans shift toward creation, oversight, and solving structured problems; AI performs highly repetitive, highly complex prediction tasks.

Task creation (Creation): AI has given rise to new roles such as “prompt engineer,” “agent commander,” and “data verifier.”

Task elimination (Elimination): Pure first–draft copywriting, junior–level coding, and basic review tasks will permanently disappear.

Rewriting the labor equation

Based on this, we must rewrite the formula for labor input:

Here, the coefficient λ (Lambda) is a core concept I propose, representing the “AI labor’s substitution/augmentation coefficient for human labor.” A company’s core competitive advantage lies in finding the steps in its business with the highest λ values and automating them, thereby freeing humans to handle high–value work where λ≈0 (such as empathy and strategic decision–making).

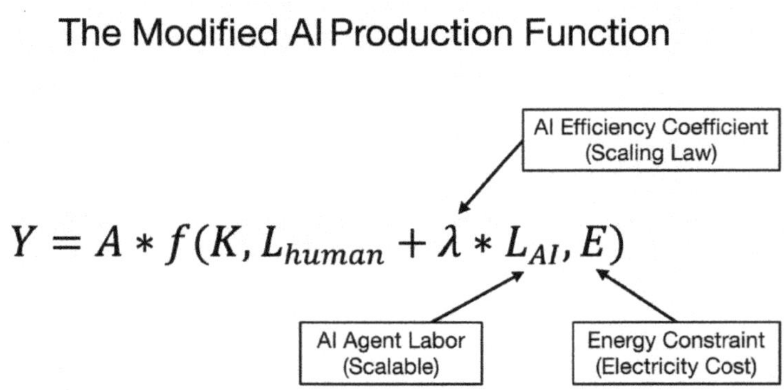

Figure 2-1 | Jason Liu - AI Economics

2.5 The revolution of capital (K): from physical capital to intelligence capital

The composition of capital is undergoing a fundamental transformation. In addition to traditional plants and machinery (physical capital), a more important form of capital is rising—Intangible Intelligence Capital (IIC). It has a unique "anti-entropy" property, whereby increased use

creates a data flywheel; the more it is used, the stronger it becomes.

But the formation of this kind of capital is not a result of free market competition. An unprecedented monopoly phenomenon is defining the supply of AI capital.

[In-depth Case] Intelligence engines: NVIDIA and the monopolistic supply of AI capital

If electricity is the lifeblood of the AI era, then high-performance GPUs are the heart of the AI era. Dingxiong Consulting's "NVIDIA 2025 Artificial Intelligence Development Strategy Research" reveals the harsh truth of this new form of capital:

Compute is power (Compute as Power):

GPU clusters are no longer ordinary IT assets; they have become national strategic infrastructure. The United States' "Stargate" program plans to invest $500 billion to build 10 GW-scale AI infrastructure, indicating that the investment threshold for K_{AI} has risen to the level of national will. The world is splitting into "compute-sovereign nations" and "compute-dependent nations."

Economics of ecosystem monopolies:

NVIDIA not only monopolizes hardware (90% market share) but has also built unfathomable economic barriers:

CUDA network effects: A software ecosystem accumulated over 16 years makes switching costs extremely high.

Full-stack lock-in: Through the "CPU+GPU+DPU" three-chip

strategy and NVLink interconnect technology, NVIDIA has raised the competitive dimension from a single chip to the system level, establishing an exclusive technical standard.

Tech–geopolitics complex:

The global allocation of AI capital no longer follows pure market–efficiency principles. U.S. export bans and the game around NVIDIA's "special edition" chips show that political power is directly distorting the supply curve of AI capital.

Conclusion: The future competition for capital is not about who has money to buy machines, but about who is qualified to obtain allocation rights to the most advanced compute.

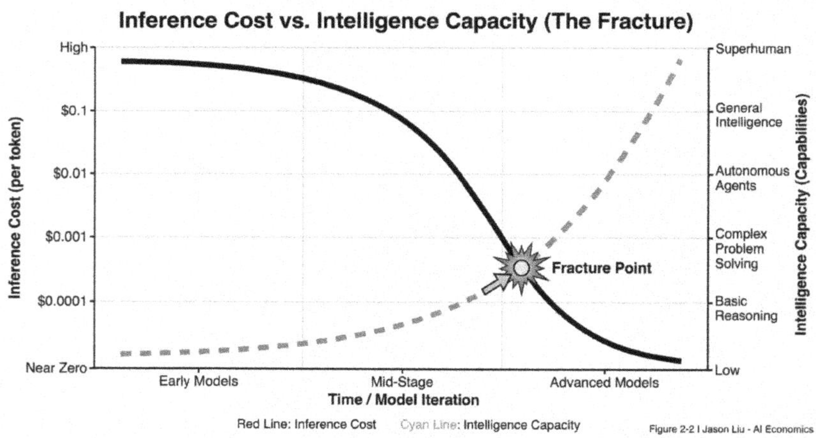

2.6 Revolution in technology (A): Endogenizing TFP and four channels

In traditional economics, technological progress (A) is usually treated as a hard–to–predict "exogenous variable." But in the AI era, A becomes an engineering problem that can be "endogenized." As long as you invest sufficient compute, data, and strong algorithms, you can "manufacture"

Driven by technological progress. AI boosts TFP primarily through the following 4 specific channels:

Reducing prediction errors (core mechanism): Much of waste in economics comes from "wrong judgments." AI performs risk identification and demand forecasting at extremely low cost.

Automating complex tasks (Automation): In automated workflows, 80% of tasks are automated, causing per-capita output to soar.

Increasing innovation speed (Innovation Elasticity): Innovation cycles shorten, and trial-and-error costs drop by 90%.

Lowering coordination costs (Coordination): AI Agent reduces managerial friction and breaks the curse of firm size.

2.7 The "intelligence-enhanced" production function and physical constraints

Putting it all together, we need a more precise mathematical model to describe the AI economy. We adopt a variant of the constant elasticity of substitution (CES) production function:

In this model, I explicitly introduce a new and crucial variable: E (Energy). This is not merely a theoretical derivation, but the most breathtaking real-world footnote to the global economy in 2024—2025.

Low-dimensional interpretation: the corrected production function

To make this seemingly complex formula easier to grasp at a glance, let's perform a dimensionality reduction interpretation:

- K (capital) has changed in meaning: In the past, firms bought machines (capital K) to assist human workers. Now, firms purchase GPU servers (the new capital K) to "hire" digital workers (L_{AI}). For the first time, capital can be directly converted into labor.

- \lambda (AI efficiency coefficient) is the critical lever: this coefficient represents a productivity ratio between an AI agent and a human employee. In certain specific tasks, the value of \lambda may be 10 or even 100. This means that for every additional unit of compute investment, the firm does not obtain a onefold increase in output, but an explosive \lambda–fold increase.
- E (energy) is the new hard constraint: As noted in the 2025 China ESG Development White Paper, the surge in data center energy consumption has become an issue that cannot be ignored. The future growth depends not only on how much compute you can obtain, but more importantly on whether you can secure sufficient, low–cost, and green energy to power that compute.

[In–Depth Case] The New Watt Era: The physical boundary of intelligent capital

According to Nomura Orient's study "The U.S. Enters a New Watt Era," we are at a historic moment when "compute power is tethered to electric power." The limit of the AI production function is not in the code, but in the grid.

Data's warning: the underestimated "snake"

Over the past decade, U.S. electricity demand grew at an average annual rate of only 0.6%, but with the AI Soared to 3.8% in 2024.

FERC projects that data center expansion alone has created a 120 GW power shortfall (equivalent to the total generation of dozens of countries). This means the physical world can no longer support the boundless expansion of the digital world.

The grid's groan: the transformer crisis

Even if power can be generated, it can't be delivered. Thirty percent of U.S. transformers are about to exceed their service life, and order backlogs at power equipment giants like Eaton have hit record highs. As a result, even if you've bought H100 GPUs, you might have to wait 2–3 years to power them up because of a missing transformer. The formation speed of intelligent capital has been locked in by aging copper wires.

The grand energy game: who will feed AI?

To break through the constraint of E, tech giants are reshaping the energy economy:

Short term: use Bloom Energy's gas turbines and SOFC for "off–grid power," bypassing congested grids.

Mid term: "PV–plus–storage integration" becomes standard, using energy storage to smooth the pulsed loads of AI training.

Ultimate solution — Nuclear Renaissance: Microsoft and Amazon are snapping up nuclear power agreements; Google is investing in OKLO's small modular reactors (SMR). Even Japan, historically most cautious about nuclear power, is restarting nuclear to address AI's power deficit.

Economic conclusion: compute is energy.

In the "New Watt Era," compute (Compute) will be rigidly exchangeable with electricity (Watt). The economic growth (Y) brought by AI (AI) will be choked off by soaring energy inflation if the supply of E is not addressed.

Chapter Summary

AI is fundamentally rewriting the "source code" of economic growth. It is no longer an exogenous technological shock, but rather, by introducing: infinitely scalable "silicon–based labor" (changing L);

"Intelligent capital" constrained by geopolitical monopolies (changing K); engineerable and manufacturable "technological progress" (endogenizing A);

it completely breaks the growth constraints of the traditional Cobb–Douglas model. At the same time, it introduces a new, more fundamental physical constraint—energy (E). The competition of the future is a competition for compute, and even more so a competition for energy.

Actionable Takeaways (Actionable Takeaways)

For business managers and decision–makers:

Calculate your company's "λ coefficient":

Take stock of core businesses and identify the segments with the highest λ values (high frequency, strong predictability, standardized) for AI substitution. This is the first step to unlocking productivity.

Examine the fragility of your supply chain:

If your business depends on high–performance compute, recognize that you are in a highly monopolized supply chain subject to geopolitical disruptions. Consider diversifying cloud providers or compute sources to mitigate "supply cut–off" risks.

Pay attention to the share of "energy costs":

In the future, when evaluating the true cost of a data center or AI project, energy costs will account for an increasing proportion. If you are a major buyer of compute, watch whether your suppliers have stable "green power" or independent energy solutions—this will determine whether your future compute costs are controllable.

Chapter 3

AI Reshapes the Labor Market: Skill Premium, Carbon-Based Premium, and the "One-Person Unicorn"

Academic positioning of this chapter: From Labor Economics to the Task–Based Model

Why is an academic degree no longer an absolute safeguard for a high salary?

When "experience" can be infinitely replicated by models, where does the core value of human labor still lie?

Before we discuss how AI reshapes employment, we need to use the lens of labor economics to understand the allocation rules behind wages and employment.

I. The Cornerstones of Traditional Labor Theory

Marginal product determines wages ($W = P \times MPL$): Traditional theory holds that a worker's wage depends on their marginal product of labor. The more value you create, the higher your wage.

Human Capital Theory: Education and training can enhance skills, thereby increasing marginal product. Therefore, "degree = skills = high salary" was an iron law of the industrial era.

Scarcity of labor (Scarcity of Labor): The labor supply is constrained by birth rates and physiological limits (people need rest), so the overall workforce is a scarce resource.

II. Revisions to traditional assumptions (the rupture brought by AI)

Correction1:Supply becomes unlimited. Intelligent agents (Agents) have broken the physical constraints that population imposes on labor supply. For tasks such as customer service, translation, and elementary coding, the labor supply curve becomes an almost flat, unlimited supply.

Revision 2: Mid–skill collapse. AI is best at replacing "rule–based symbolic processing tasks." (i.e., white–collar work). This accelerates the labor market's shift from an "olive–shaped" distribution to a "K–shaped" one—the middle is hollowed out, while the upper tier is exponentially strengthened.

Revision 3: Reconstructing skill premiums. The premium on academic credentials is giving way to "AI leverage." In the future, high salaries will no longer be paid to "people who possess knowledge," but to "people who can direct AI to draw on knowledge."

III. Forward-Looking Case: Klarna's 700-Person Replacement Experiment

To validate the "middle–skill collapse," we turn to the fintech giant Klarna.

In 2024, Klarna's AI customer service system independently handled 2/3 of customer interactions (equivalent to the workload of 700 full–time employees), reducing resolution time from 11 minutes to 2 minutes.

This is not simply a matter of layoffs, but a complete rewrite of task structures: humans move away from repetitive Retreat from Q&A, pivot to handling complex disputes and emotional reassurance (carbon–based premium).

3.0 Introduction: AI is not "stealing jobs," but "redefining jobs."

Discussions about AI and employment often fall into the binary opposition of "replacement" versus "creation."

But the reality is far more complicated than that.

AI is carrying out a fine-grained "skill repricing" of the labor market. It is not simply eliminating jobs; it is mercilessly punishing the "mediocre" while wildly rewarding the "scarce." It is tearing the labor market into two extreme dimensions.

3.1 Traditional economic framework: the underlying logic of wages and employment

(The Logic of Labor: Traditional Framework)

Labor economics focuses on the two most central questions in the entire economic system: How is labor priced (wages)? How is labor allocated (employment)? To address these, traditional economics has built a mature theory that explains the labor structure of industrial society over the past two hundred years.

(1) The determination of wages: a game of supply and demand

Wages are not set at the whim of the boss; they are determined by market supply and demand.

- Labor supply (Supply): typically upward sloping. The higher the wage, the more people are willing to work (or the longer they are willing to work). It is influenced by population size, education level, and social culture (such as female labor force participation).
- Labor demand (Demand): typically downward sloping. The higher the wage, the fewer people firms are willing to hire. It is influenced by the level of technology and product market demand.

The intersection of the two forms the market equilibrium wage.

(2) Marginal Product (MPL): The yardstick of capability

How much a company is willing to pay depends on how much value an employee can create. In economics, this is called the Marginal Product of Labor (MPL).

That is: Wage (W) = Product Price (P) × Marginal Product of Labor (MPL)

- The reason a top programmer earns more than an assembly line worker is that he creates higher–value code (MPL) per unit of time.
- This logic explains the economic foundation of "distribution according to labor": your output determines your income.

(3) Human Capital Theory (Human Capital Theory)

Nobel laureate Gary Becker (Gary Becker) proposed Human Capital Theory as a cornerstone for explaining income disparities. He argued that workers can invest in themselves to raise MPL, thereby earning higher wages.

- Forms of investment: education, training, experience accumulation, and maintaining health.
- Core inference: Income gap ≈ skills/education gap. In the industrial era, this led to the social consensus that "going to college = a good job." Higher educational attainment generally implies higher human capital and higher marginal product.

(4) Labor stratification: an olive-shaped social structure

Traditional labor economics divides workers into three categories by skill, forming a stable social structure:

- High–skill labor: analysis, creation, management (e.g., lawyers, doctors, executives). High wages.
- Mid–skill labor: routine, processable white–collar and blue–collar work (e.g., accountants, administrative staff, assembly line supervisors). This is the backbone of the middle class.
- Low–skill labor: physically demanding and service–oriented jobs

(e.g., cleaning, food service).

In the past few decades, mid–skill workers have accounted for the largest share, forming a stable "olive–shaped" society.

(5) Types of unemployment: it's not just about not having a job

Economics classifies unemployment into three types:

- Frictional unemployment: the gap period between jobs (a normal phenomenon).
- Cyclical unemployment: layoffs caused by economic crises (a short–term phenomenon).
- Structural unemployment: the most dangerous type. It refers to a mismatch between workers' skills and market demand (for example, coachmen becoming unemployed in the automobile era). Technological progress often brings short–term structural unemployment, but traditional theory holds that in the long run technology creates more new jobs.

Summarizing the traditional framework: The labor logic of the industrial era is: population determines supply, skills determine wages, education changes one's fate, and the middle class is the stabilizer of society. This is a logic based on "linear growth in human capabilities."

3.2 Overview of Changes in the AI Era: The K-shaped Rewrite of Labor Structure

(The Rewrite: How AI Redefines Work)

AI has not overturned labor economics, but it has recalibrated every key variable within the above framework, resulting in a rupture in the labor structure.

(1) Labor supply curve rewritten: The addition of silicon–based labor is the largest supply–side shock in 100 years.

- Traditional: L=ext{ population }imesext{ labor force participation rate }.

- AI: L_{ext{eff}}=L_{ext{human}}+\lambda\cdot L {ext{AI}}. We must incorporate "AI labor" into the supply function. AI agents, as endlessly replicable and tireless labor, vastly increase the supply of certain tasks (such as entry-level coding, translation, customer service), causing wages in these areas to face substantial downward pressure.

(2) Reconstruction of skill premium: AI literacy and educational attainment—human capital theory still holds,

but the definition of "capital" has changed.

- In the past: income gap = educational attainment gap.
- Now: Income gap = Skills gap × AI leverage (AI Literacy). An undergraduate who knows how to use AI tools may have a marginal product of labor (MPL) far exceeding that of a PhD who does not understand AI. The premium on educational credentials is being diluted by the "AI usage premium."

(3) Mid-skill collapse and K-shaped polarization. AI is best at "rule-based symbolic processing tasks," which happen to be the core work of the middle class (accounting, auditing, junior analysis).

- Mid-skill: massively replaced by AI, facing the risk of "downward drift" or "unemployment."
- High-skill: amplified by AI, with income rising further.
- Low-skill: because it involves non-standard physical environments (such as fixing pipes, hairdressing), it is relatively safe in the short term. This drives the social structure to evolve from an "olive-shaped" distribution to a "K-shaped" (polarized) one.

(4) Synergy in marginal product of labor. In the AI era, MPL is no longer calculated on a solo basis.

In the future, high pay will no longer go to "people who can complete tasks," but to "people who can direct AI to complete tasks." Humans and AI have a multiplicative relationship, not an additive one.

(5) Updating the definition of unemployment: Task vs Job. The "task model" proposed by MIT economist Daron Acemoglu has become the mainstream lens. AI will not directly eliminate an entire "job" (e.g., designer), but it will replace most of the "tasks" within that job (e.g., retouching, typesetting). The essence of unemployment becomes "task stripping": if 90% of the tasks in your job can be done by AI, the job will disappear; if only 20% are replaced, you will instead get a raise thanks to efficiency gains.

3.3 Deep case: Klarna

(Case Study: The Great Restructuring of Middle–Skill Labor)

To demonstrate that the "collapse of middle–skill jobs" is not alarmist, we introduce Europe's largest finan The real–world case of fintech unicorn Klarna. This may be the clearest labor–substitution experiment globally in 2024. (Data sources: Klarna official press release 2024/CNBC/Financial Times)

I. Background: A typical medium–skill labor–intensive department. As a payments company serving 150 million users worldwide, Klarna has a large customer service team. Customer service work is a typical form of "medium–skill labor":

- Task characteristics: high repetitiveness, rule–based, involving extensive text handling and process judgments (such as refunds and balance inquiries).
- Cost structure: reliant on large amounts of manpower, with high training costs and response speed constrained by staffing levels.

II. AI intervention: Structural displacement of labor. In early 2024, Klarna announced that an AI customer service system powered by OpenAI was officially launched, fully taking over customer interactions. This is not simple auto–reply, but an intelligent agent with capabilities in understanding, decision–making, and execution.

III. Quantitative results: Stunning substitution rate

- Workload substitution: AI independently handled 2/3 of customer service interactions (equivalent to the workload of 700 full–time employees).
- Efficiency transformation: the average time to resolve customer issues was reduced from 11 minutes to 2 minutes.
- Quality on par: Customer satisfaction scores are on par with those of human customer service.
- Financial impact: It is expected to add $40 million in profit for the company in 2024.

IV. Economic Insights: Klarna's case is a microcosm of a new chapter in labor economics:

1. Task substitution: AI has precisely stripped out the "information–based repetitive processing" tasks within customer service roles.

2. Hiring Freeze: Klarna did not carry out large–scale layoffs but announced it would shrink the team through Attrition and a hiring freeze. This means "entry–level, middle–skill positions" are closing their doors to young people.

3. Value shift: Human employees are forced (or freed) to handle the very small number of complex disputes and emotional soothing tasks that AI cannot resolve—this is the embodiment of the "carbon–based premium."

3.4 The Industrial Revolution replaced physical strength; the AI revolution replaces brainpower.

Traditional technological advances (steam engines, electric motors) have always replaced "manual labor" or "repetitive mechanical skills." AI, however, is the first technology to directly impact "cognitive labor": What AI replaces is not the hand, but the brain.

In particular, copywriting, preparing PPTs, data analysis, market forecasting, preliminary financial review, recruitment Screening for recruitment, preliminary legal intake, and similar tasks. In essence, these tasks are "prediction + rules + judgment," which is exactly what AI excels at. Therefore, AI's impact on the labor market is not gradual; it directly targets the core roles of the middle class.

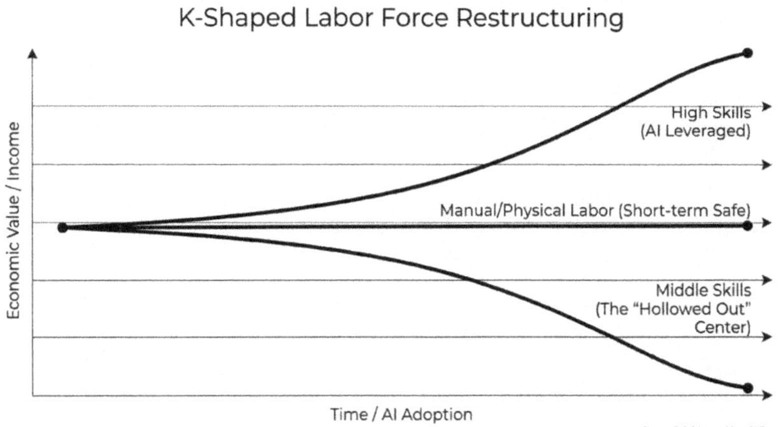

Figure 3-2 | Jason Liu - AI Economics

3.5 Task Model: AI replaces "tasks," not "occupations."

The "Task Model" proposed by Acemoglu and Restrepo is the most precise framework for analyzing AI's employment impact. The traditional view that "AI will replace certain occupations" is incorrect. What AI has always replaced are tasks, not occupations.

Case: The deconstruction of the real estate agent

A real estate agent's occupation consists of many tasks: writing property listings, conducting market analysis, appraisals, drafting contracts, maintaining social media, arranging viewings, and negotiating with clients.

Among these, the first 70% of tasks (copywriting, analysis, appraisal, drafting) can all be automated by AI.

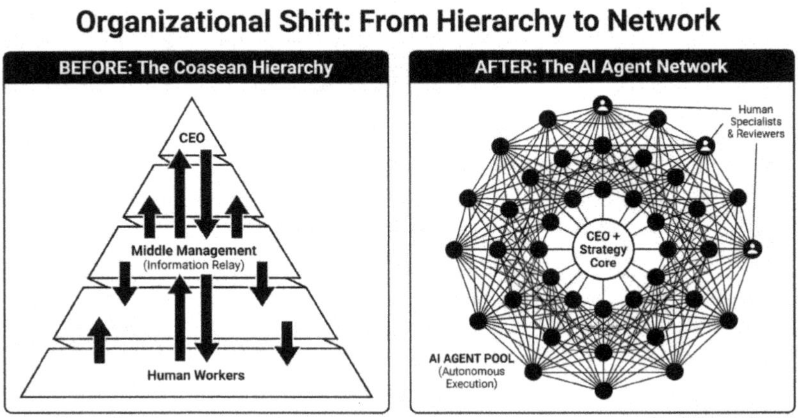

Figure 4-1 | Jason Liu - AI Economics

Therefore, what AI brings is not "job disappearance," but rather: jobs are unbundled →some tasks are taken over by AI → the content of the occupation changes. Automation index: Which tasks are most easily replaced?

Tasks based on symbols and language: contract drafting, copywriting, code generation. LLMs have an overwhelming inherent advantage.

Tasks based on structured information: financial analysis, initial recruitment screening, risk control review.

Tasks with clear processes and rules: expense approval, order processing, customer follow–up. These are the home turf of AI Agents.

3.6 Exponential amplification of the Skill Premium: K-shaped divergence

AI is becoming a "super–leverage" for top talent. A top–tier programmer, designer, or strategist can readily boost output efficiency by 5–10x with AI assistance. A mid–level professional may only achieve a 1.5–2x increase. This efficiency gap will directly lead to an exponential widening of income disparities.

The middle class is most at risk: validation of the Autor–Weilson model

AI is the first to simultaneously impact low–, medium–, and high–skill labor, but with sharply different effects:

Low–skill workers (relatively safe): cleaners, caregivers, blue–collar workers. Because their tasks are unstructured and rely on physical operations, they are hard to replace in the short term.

Mid–skill workers (highest risk): mid–level clerks, junior accountants, junior programmers, administrative staff, middle managers. The task structures of these roles are most suitable for AI automation. Middle–class incomes will face substantial squeeze.

High–skill workers (the strong get stronger): top lawyers, doctors, entrepreneurs. AI as an "intelligent assistant" will significantly raise their efficiency.

Conclusion: The income polarization trend driven by AI is— the poor will not necessarily get poorer, the middle class is at greater risk, and the rich will get richer.

3.7 Carbon-based Premium (Carbon-based Premium): When the "human touch" becomes a luxury

This is a counterintuitive yet crucial concept. When AI (silicon–based intelligence) can deliver massive, standardized intelligent services at extremely low cost, those "carbon–based services" that cannot be replicated by AI and that rely heavily on human physical presence and emotional connection will instead see their value rise sharply.

In the future, high–paying roles will concentrate in four domains with high "carbon–based premiums":

Building deep trust and emotional connection: the listening of psychotherapists, the hand–holding of hospice nurses, and the presence of private bankers during moments of family crisis.

Assuming ultimate responsibility and moral judgment: in ethical dilemmas of autonomous driving or life–and–death choices in major business strategy, the "responsible agent" is an inalienable human attribute.

Handling extremely unstructured information and cross–domain association: entrepreneurs sensing opportunity amid chaotic signals, or artists creating new genres.

Bodily craftsmanship and sense of presence: on–site cooking by Michelin–star chefs, the techniques of traditional Chinese medicine massage therapists.

3.8 Changes in wage structure: rewriting the formula

Future wage structures will no longer depend on "experience," but on the "AI leverage ratio":

W_H: human's own capability

W_{AI}: capability to leverage AI

θ: AI usage efficiency coefficient

This means: In the future, the highest–paid roles won't be "people who can do things," but "people who can use AI to get things done."

3.9 Job restructuring: the rise of the "atomization" of work and the "project-based" model

The traditional concept of a "job" is being eroded. AI enables companies to break complex projects into "task atoms" that can be completed independently by AI or by humans (Task Atom).

For companies: no longer hire a full–time "marketing manager," but dynamically combine an "AI strategist + human creative director."

For individuals: work becomes "taking on projects." Individuals will become a “company of one,” plugging into value networks around their core skills.

3.10 The birth of the “Unicorn of One”

This is the boldest prediction of this chapter. Empowered by AI, we will witness “companies of one” creating business value that previously required teams of hundreds.

AI Legion Commander Mode:

The future is not AI replacing humans, but AI giving everyone a “digital labor legion.”

Real estate agents: Backed by 10 AI agents (valuation, copywriting, contracts, marketing, order follow–up). The agent personally handles only core communication and strategy. This is exactly the direction of Longmei Real Estate’s AI full–stack strategy.

Programmers: AI writes code, debugs, and tests; humans do architecture design and reviews.

CEO: No longer managing “people,” but managing an “AI chain of command.”

Chapter Summary

The labor market in the AI era is a world of extremes—ice and fire.

It ruthlessly eliminates “standardizable middle skills” (such as basic customer service, junior coding, and routine translation), while lavishly rewarding two types of people:

1. Top talent who can harness AI and command algorithmic legions;
2. Providers of “carbon–based premium” services that offer deep emotional connection and involve complex physical operations.

Actionable Takeaways (Actionable Takeaways)

For every individual who wants to remain competitive in the age of intelligence:

1. Undertake a "skills hedging" exercise:

Examine the most time–consuming and repetitive parts of your current job. If these tasks can be clearly described as a series of "if not... then..." rules, they carry a very high risk of being replaced by AI within 3 years. You must proactively exit these areas and learn higher–order abstraction skills.

2. Build your "human-in-the-loop" system:

Don't treat AI as a simple search tool; treat it as your "copilot." Deliberately practice a workflow where AI produces the first draft (0 to 1), and then you perform the optimization, judgment, and decision–making (1 to 100).

3. Find your "carbon-based premium":

If you're not good at dealing with machines (logic/code), then double down on your ability to deal with people (empathy/communication/negotiation). In an era when everyone is staring at screens, a warm smile and a sincere handshake may be worth more than a line of perfect code.

Chapter 4

AI Reshapes the Boundaries of the Firm: The End of Coase's Theorem and the "Intelligence Tax"

Academic positioning of this chapter: From Transaction Cost Theory to the Agentic Network Model

Why do firms exist, rather than everyone working as freelancers? Why can't firms expand indefinitely and must be constrained by managerial hierarchies?

Before we enter the discussion of how AI reshapes organizations, we need to use the lens of New Institutional Economics to understand the underlying equation behind firm boundaries.

I. The Cornerstones of Traditional Organizational Theory

Coase Theorem: The existence of firms is to resolve market "frictions." When internal management costs are lower than external market transaction costs (search, negotiation, contracting), firm boundaries expand.

Bounded Rationality: Due to the limited cognitive bandwidth of human managers, one person can typically manage effectively 8–12 people. This leads to the inevitability of the "golden pyramid bureaucracy" — to manage scale, layers must be added.

Internal Coordination Costs: As a firm grows, information distortion and slower decision processes cause internal costs to rise exponentially, thereby locking in the firm's maximum size.

II. Revisions to traditional assumptions (the rupture brought by AI)

Revision 1: Parameters reduced to zero. AI simultaneously pierces "external transaction costs" (extremely fast search and matching) and "internal management costs" (automated communication and oversight). The formula that once maintained the equilibrium of firm boundaries fails, pushing organizations to extremes — either very small (one–person companies) or very large (platform monopolies).

Revision 2: Structural liquefaction. The "human brain bandwidth limit" that supports pyramid structures is broken. Agents take over coordination and supervision, dissolving firms from a solid hierarchical structure into a "liquid network of intelligent agents."

Revision 3: Management radius explosion. AI's full audit and automatic task dispatch capabilities boost a manager's effective span of control from 10 people to 100 or more, posing an unprecedented challenge to the value of middle managers.

III. Forward-Looking Case: BBVA's 3,000-Agent Experiment

To validate "organizational liquefaction," we analyze the banking giant BBVA.

In a vast hierarchical organization with 120,000 employees, BBVA deployed 3,000 AI agents to take over core processes such as legal preliminary review and compliance auditing, achieving symbiosis between 120,000 people and silicon–based employees.

This is not merely an efficiency boost; it is a physical reshaping of the boundaries of enterprise operations.

4.0 Introduction: From the Coase Theorem to the Limits of Agility

In 1937, Nobel laureate in economics Ronald Coase raised a fundamental question: if markets can efficiently allocate resources through the price mechanism, why do firms need to exist?

His answer was: because markets involve "transaction costs," such as searching for suppliers, negotiating prices, and signing contracts. The essence of the firm is to replace external market transactions with internal administrative directives, thereby reducing these costs. The boundary of the firm lies at the point where internal management costs equal external transaction costs.

Over the past two decades, faced with an increasingly volatile market environment, traditional large enterprises have undertaken "agile transformations" to reduce their increasingly bloated internal management costs. The White Paper on Large–Scale Agile Practices in Chinese Enterprises by 2025 documents this process in detail. However, although agile practices have, to some extent, increased organizational responsiveness, they are still built on a human–centered collaboration model, constrained by human communication bandwidth and cognitive coordination capacity.

But in the AI era, the two foundations of Coase's theorem—external transaction costs and internal management costs—are being punctured simultaneously.

4.1 The traditional theoretical framework of the firm: the logic of Coase's theorem and the pyramid

(Why Firms Exist: The Coasean Framework)

Before we examine how AI is disrupting enterprises, we must first answer the most essential question: why does the firm exist? In the perfect assumptions of classical economics, the market has an "invisible hand" that regulates everything. If the market were perfect, then every

Any individual can be an independent sole proprietor, completing all production through market transactions: if you need to build a car, you go to the market to buy parts, hire labor, purchase designs, and then assemble them. But in reality, we see large organizations—enterprises. Why?

(1) Coase Theorem: The "friction" of the market

In 1937, Ronald Coase proposed a groundbreaking idea in "The Nature of the Firm": using the market entails costs. These are the well-known transaction costs. (Transaction Costs).

- Search costs: you need to spend time finding who sells the parts and who offers the lowest price.
- Bargaining costs: you need to haggle with every parts supplier and every worker, signing hundreds of contracts.
- Enforcement and monitoring costs: you need to keep an eye on whether everyone delivers on time, and if there's a breach, you have to go to court.

The logic of the firm's existence: To avoid the high costs of market transactions, entrepreneurs choose to "bring these people inside" and sign long-term employment contracts. Within the firm, "prices" no longer direct actions; "authority (commands)" does. Conclusion: When internal management costs < external transaction costs, firms arise, and their boundaries keep expanding until the two become equal.

(2) The pyramid structure: a compromise of human cognition

Since firms can reduce transaction costs, why don't they expand without limit? Why isn't there a single "super company" for the whole world? Because as firms grow larger, Internal Coordination Costs rise sharply:

- Information distortion: as directives move from the CEO to the frontline, information attenuates layer by layer.

- Decision paralysis: the more layers there are, the slower the approvals.
- Span of Control limitation: management research shows that a single manager's effective management radius is usually only 8–12 people.

To solve this problem, humans invented "Hierarchy," the pyramid structure we're familiar with:

This structure is not meant to oppress, but to enable collaboration at the scale of tens of thousands under humans' limited cognitive bandwidth. It was the optimal solution for organizational efficiency in the industrial era.

(3) The "five major costs" of internal corporate operations

To understand the impact of AI precisely, we need to further break down a firm's "internal management costs" into five dimensions. These five costs are what lock in the efficiency ceiling of traditional enterprises:

1. Communication costs (Communication): the time consumed by meetings, emails, and document circulation.

2. Coordination costs (Coordination): friction in cross–department alignment, schedule synchronization, and resource allocation.

3. Monitoring costs (Monitoring): KPI assessments, process approvals, and ensuring employees don't slack off.

4. Decision–making costs (Decision–Making): the process of gathering information, analyzing data, and making judgments.

5. Execution cost (Execution): the human effort required to turn decisions into concrete actions.

Summary of the traditional framework: the firm is a product of "using management to replace the market." Its boundaries are determined by the game between transaction costs and management costs, and its structure (pyramid) is determined by the cognitive limits of human managers.

4.2 Overview of changes in the AI era: parameter reset to zero and structural liquefaction

(The Rewrite: Zero–Cost Coordination)

AI has not overturned the logic of Coase's theorem (the logic of cost comparison), but it has caused a discontinuous change in the parameter values on both sides of the equation.

(1) Internal communication costs: from "high" to "very low"

- Traditional: information transmission relies on layer–by–layer reporting, document writing, and lengthy meetings. There is severe "information noise" and "transmission delay."
- AI: large models possess strong semantic understanding and generation capabilities. Meeting minutes are auto–generated, real–time cross–language translation, automatic document summarization, and automatic extraction of tacit knowledge. Communication is no longer the hauling of information, but its "instant synchronization."

(2) Coordination costs: automatic orchestration by intelligent agents

- Traditional: a large number of middle managers (Middle Management) are needed to act as "human routers," responsible for distributing tasks and chasing progress.
- AI: Intelligent agents (Agents) can autonomously break down tasks, call tools across systems automatically, and automatically track progress. Coordination shifts from "human–to–human" to "Agent–to–Agent."

(3) Supervision costs: from "human monitoring" to "digital auditing"

- Traditional: relies on time clocks, weekly reports, and KPI interviews.
- AI: Behavior logs (Audit Logs) replace manual oversight. AI

can analyze complete work data in real time to identify risks and assess quality. Supervision becomes invisible yet all–encompassing, and the span of control expands from 10 people to 100 or even more.

(4) Decision-making and execution: restructuring the division of labor between humans and machines

- AI does prediction (Prediction): processes massive datasets to provide the probabilistically optimal solution.
- AI does execution (Execution): generates content, code, and reports.
- Humans exercise judgment (Judgment): make the final choice based on AI's predictions and assume responsibility. Decision chains shorten, and execution costs drop by 50%—90%.

(5) Result: The pyramid collapses, agent networks rise. Due to the sharp decline in the above costs, the economic foundation supporting the "pyramidal structure" no longer exists.

- De–layering: middle managers responsible for relaying information and supervising are replaced by AI.
- Expansion of enterprise boundaries: The scale of business that a single core team can manage grows exponentially.
- Organizational liquidization: the enterprise is no longer a fixed hierarchy, but a fluid organization of a "core human team + dynamic AI agent network."

4.3 In-depth case: BBVA (Banco Bilbao Vizcaya Argentaria)

(Case Study: The Fluid Organization in Banking)

To show how "rewriting corporate boundaries" happens in reality, we take a deep look at the global digital benchmark in banking—BBVA. (Data sources: BBVA official annual reports / OpenAI Enterprise Case Study / Microsoft Azure)

I. Background: A typical Coasean giant BBVA is a top–tier European financial group with 125,000 employees in over 30 countries. As a heavily regulated, process–intensive bank, it has the classic feature of "high internal coordination costs":

- Vast amounts of compliance reviews;
- Complex cross–border legal processes;
- Millions of manual customer inquiries. According to traditional theory, keeping such a massive machine running must rely on a heavy bureaucratic hierarchy.

II. AI intervention: Building an "enterprise–grade agent network" 2023–2024, BBVA has implemented a radical AI transformation across the entire bank, deploying an enterprise–grade brain based on GPT–4. This is not merely a tool upgrade, but a reconstruction of organizational logic:

- Agent deployment: More than 3,000 customized AI agents have been deployed, covering core functions such as Legal, Audit, Risk Management, and IT Development.
- Universal access: 125,000 employees have been granted the right to invoke AI compute, forming a "human + AI" hybrid workflow.

III. Quantified Results: Breaking Boundaries

- Process automation: In Legal and Compliance, AI agents have taken over initial document reviews, improving efficiency by 4–6 times. This means the bank can manage a larger asset base with fewer people.
- Service boundary expansion: The AI customer service system has successfully offloaded 70% of routine inquiries and can handle 24/7 multilingual support. The bank's service capacity is no longer constrained by branch headcount.
- Knowledge internalization: Query and utilization rates of the internal knowledge base have risen to over 80%, and the Onboarding (入职培训) cycle for new employees has been

significantly shortened.

IV. Economic Insights: BBVA's case is a dynamic interpretation of the Coase Theorem in the AI era:

1. Internal costs plunge: AI has dramatically reduced the bank's internal coordination and execution costs.

2. Expanded management radius: The core management team can now directly oversee global operations via AI dashboards and agent networks, breaking through the information barriers of the middle layer.

3. Organizational liquefaction: Banks are transforming from rigid bureaucratic institutions into agile platforms that are "data-driven, compute-executed."

4.4 AI is fundamentally reducing the six most important costs for enterprises

The emergence of AI technologies (LLM, Agent, Workflow) is launching a simultaneous attack on two dimensions: it dramatically lowers transaction costs in external markets while also greatly reducing internal management and coordination costs. This is causing an unprecedented shift in corporate cost structures.

What AI is reducing is not the cost of a single department, but the six core costs on which the essence of the enterprise depends:

Prediction cost (Prediction): the core value of AI. Which customers will buy? What price is most reasonable? AI has turned prediction into a near-zero-cost activity, reconstructing the entire decision-making system.

Communication cost (Communication): in the past, a manager spent 40% of their time on communication; now AI auto-generates reports, summarizes meetings, and drafts emails, driving communication costs to a minimum.

Coordination cost (Coordination): among intelligent agents, tasks can be automatically allocated, documents proofread, and processes executed. For the first time, companies can use an "agent chain" to replace expensive human management chains.

Supervision cost (Supervision): AI can run 7x24 in the background to check processes, risks, and compliance. In the past, 5 supervisors monitored 50 people; in the future, 1 AI can monitor 500 people.

Learning cost (Learning): the more human employees, the higher the training costs, but AI becomes smarter the longer it is used. This is a reverse logic: the marginal cost of experience accumulation is negative.

Execution cost (Execution): shifting from "decide → assign tasks → humans execute" to "deci– sion → AI Agent executes directly."

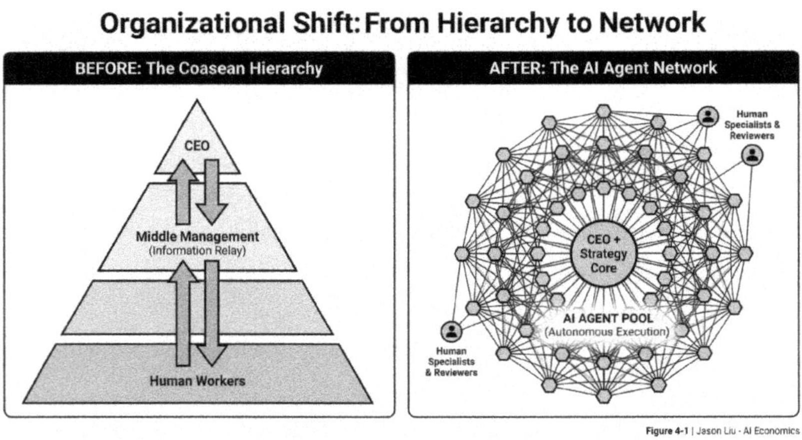

4.5 The "dissolution" and "liquefaction" of corporate boundaries

When external transaction costs fall below internal management costs, a firm's boundaries begin to "dissolve."

Search and negotiation costs approach zero: AI Agent can identify the optimal solution from millions of global suppliers within milliseconds and simulate millions of games to secure the best contract.

Supervision costs approach zero: Smart contracts and the Internet of Things automatically trigger penalties for breaches.

This drives organizational forms to evolve from a solid, hierarchical bureaucracy into a liquid network of intelligent agents network.

Result: Traditional "giant dinosaur" enterprises with tens of thousands of employees will be replaced by "agile starfish" networks composed of a small core team and a large array of external AI services and human experts. A company's core competitiveness will no longer be "how many employees it has," but "how much external intelligence it can connect and orchestrate."

4.6 The shape of the firm: from a pyramid to an "intelligent agent network"

The past organizational structure was pyramidal: CEO\rightarrow executives \rightarrow

middle management \rightarrow frontline.

The organizational structure in the AI era is networked: CEO\rightarrow human strike team (10 people) \rightarrow AI intelligent agent network (100—1000 units).

The organizations of the future take on an entirely new shape:

Flattened (Flat): Middle management is drastically reduced. Because AI takes on coordination, control, aggregation, and allocation tasks, middle management positions may decrease by 50%–80%.

Networked (Networked): The enterprise operates as an "automated neural network." It is no longer a "human → human" assembly line, but an "AI → AI → AI → human" intelligent chain.

Modular (Modular): The organization is no longer divided into departments, but into agent modules (Sales Agent, Finance Agent, Legal

Agent). This gives the company unprecedented Lego–like flexibility.

4.7 Future organizational prototype: "10 people + 100 agents"

The most successful companies of the future will no longer be massive enterprises with thousands of employees, but rather:

10 human core members + 100 AI agents + automated workflows = the output of a traditional 300– person company.

Real–world case: AI full–stack real estate company

Luxmore Realty (Canada) AI strategy is a real–world application of this model:

AI performs CMA (valuation)

AI does customer engagement and marketing

AI handles ad distribution and copywriting

AI drafts contracts and manages risk control

Human core team: focused on strategy, emotional connection, and complex negotiations. This isn't just about cutting costs and boosting efficiency; it's "building a company from the future back to the present."

4.8 New "gatekeepers" and the "Intelligence Tax" (Intelligence Tax)

However, this does not herald a fully decentralized utopia. As companies outsource more and more of their core operations to external AI platforms or internal AI models, they are, often unknowingly, placing their fate in the hands of new "gatekeepers" — the tech giants that provide the foundational large models and compute power (such as OpenAI, Google, Microsoft, NVIDIA).

Intelligence Tax:

I call this dependency the "Intelligence Tax." In the future, most corporate profits will be paid upward to these underlying AI infrastructure providers in the form of API call fees, compute subscriptions, and platform service fees. Much like "rent" in the era of commercial real estate, it will become a fixed cost that no company can avoid.

4.9 A company's core value proposition: from "production" to "curation"

In an era when everyone can tap powerful AI, a company's value is no longer in "production" itself (because production capability has become cheap), but in "curation" (Curation) and "trust" (Trust).

Curation: From a vast array of options generated by AI, select, combine, and customize the solutions most suitable for specific customer segments.

Trust: When AI can generate anything, "authenticity" and "reliability" become extremely scarce. A trustworthy brand will serve as the most important beacon for consumers in an ocean of information.

Chapter Summary

AI is bringing an end to the world described by the Coase theorem.

By dismantling six core costs (prediction, communication, coordination, supervision, learning, execution), it turns firm boundaries from solid to liquid, transparent, and permeable. The corporate form shifts from a "pyramid" to an "agent network," the middle layer disappears, and organizations become extremely flat.

But this has not brought complete liberation; instead, it has shaped a new and more powerful center—AI platforms. For companies to survive in the future, they must evolve from "producers" to "curators" and learn to cope with the unavoidable "intelligence tax."

Actionable Takeaways (Actionable Takeaways)

For corporate strategists:

Cut your "middle layer":

Examine your org chart. Those middle management layers that only "relay orders up and down" and "coordinate communication" are the first to be optimized in the AI era. Decisively replace them with more efficient collaboration software and AI project assistants.

Embrace "liquefaction" and "in-house outsourcing":

Consider this question: Which operations can be "in–house outsourced" via AI Agents? (e.g., AI legal, AI accounting). Use ultra–low costs to "outsource to the inside" many tasks AI".

Stay vigilant (against the intelligence tax):

When choosing your AI tech stack, keep it as flexible as possible. Avoid being "locked in" to a single platform or vendor. Try to build a multi–cloud strategy to ensure you have the ability to "swap out the engine" at any time.

Build your "10+100" model:

Don't try to hire more people; instead, try to add more Agents. Start designing your first "digital employee" and let it take over a complete business closed loop.

Chapter 5

AI Reshaping Management: From "Carrot + Stick" to the "Inverted-Nail Organization"

Academic positioning of this chapter: From the Information Processing View to Agentic Orchestration

Is the essence of management about managing people, or about processing information?

When AI can distribute tasks and supervise progress more efficiently than human managers, does the pyramid structure still have a reason to exist?

Before we delve into how AI reshapes management, we need to use the lenses of managerial economics and organizational behavior to understand the compromises and inevitabilities behind bureaucracy.

I. The Cornerstones of Traditional Management Theory

Bounded Rationality and Information Filtering (Bounded Rationality): Nobel laureate Herbert Simon pointed out that management exists to overcome the human brain's limitations in processing information. The pyramid structure is essentially a man-made "information compression and transmission network"—the purpose of the middle layer is to filter information and prevent overload at the top.

Span of Control (Span of Control): Constrained by attention and energy, a human manager can typically manage only 8–12 people effectively. To manage large organizations, companies have had to stack management layers, resulting in lengthy decision chains.

Agency Cost and Supervision (Agency Cost): To prevent employees from slacking off or committing fraud, companies must establish costly KPI evaluation and manual supervision systems.

II. Revisions to traditional assumptions (the rupture brought by AI)

Revision 1: Cognitive bandwidth becomes unlimited. AI breaks the "Simon constraint." Large models can instantly read all frontline logs and customer recordings and provide decision recommendations, eliminating the need for the middle layer as an information relay. The CEO can directly reach the frontline.

Revision 2: Coordination at zero cost. Agents take over task distribution, progress tracking, and cross–department alignment. Coordination costs shift from exponential growth to near zero, and internal organizational friction disappears.

Revision 3: Explosive management radius. System–level supervision based on Audit Logs replaces "person–to–person monitoring." This increases a manager's effective span of control from 10 people to 100 people or even more, pushing the organization toward an "inverted nail" structure.

III. Forward-Looking Case: Walmart's coordination of 2.1 million people

To validate "ultra–large–scale automated management," we analyze the retail giant Walmart.

In a complex system with 2.1 million employees, AI has taken over supply chain forecasting, automated scheduling, and even procurement negotiations with suppliers. This proves that AI is no longer just an auxiliary tool, but is becoming a "second layer of management" for enterprises.

5.0 Introduction: The Century-long Crisis of Management and the Essence of Information

From Taylor's scientific management to Drucker, the past century of management theory has been built on a basic assumption: managers are smarter and better informed than employees. The core job of managers is to break down top-level strategic intent into bottom-level tasks, and supervise execution through the "carrot + stick."

Peter Drucker once pointed out: "The essence of management is the organization of information, not personnel arrangements."

Before AI, information was collected by employees, analyzed by managers, and decisions were made by executives, and execution was carried out by the organization. Therefore, companies had to rely on hierarchies, departments, and reporting lines to keep running. But AI is rendering this invisible foundation completely ineffective.

5.1 The Traditional Managerial Economics Framework: The Inevitability of the Pyramid

(The Economics of Management: Why Hierarchy Exists)

Over the past hundred-plus years, whether in Taylor's scientific management, Fayol's general management theory, or Drucker's management by objectives, "management" as a field of practice has essentially always revolved around three core actions:

1. Coordinate: Get everyone in step.

2. Decide: Make choices under uncertainty.

3. Monitor & Incentivize: Ensure tasks get done. Why do all traditional enterprises, whether in China or abroad, ultimately take the

shape of a "pyramid"?

What does it look like? Because before the advent of AI, we were constrained by three underlying economic assumptions:

(1) Information is scarce, expensive, and slow-moving

Nobel laureate Herbert Simon believed that the essence of management Its essence is "processing information." In traditional enterprises, market information, customer feedback, and production data are all scattered at the grassroots level. To enable senior management to make decisions, hierarchies must be established to "filter" and "transmit" information.

- If mid-level managers didn't write weekly reports, make PPTs, and brief in meetings, the CEO would be swamped by a deluge of raw data.
- A pyramid structure is, in essence, a manually constructed "information compression and transmission network."

(2) Coordination costs rise exponentially with scale

As companies grow larger, the friction coefficient between departments increases exponentially.

- The Sales Department sold the goods, but the factory didn't know; the Finance Department deducted the payment, but the Purchasing Department didn't know.
- To resolve the chaos, companies must introduce processes, meetings, and dedicated coordinators (Middle management). This led to the "big-company disease" in large enterprises: to coordinate the work of 1 person, it might require 0.5 managers. The surge in coordination costs locked in the upper limit of corporate expansion.

(3) Supervision relies on the "human eye," incurring agency costs

How can we ensure employees don't slack off or commit fraud? Traditional management relies on "person-to-person supervision."

- Set supervisors to keep a close watch on employees;
- Appoint managers to keep an eye on supervisors;
- Set up audits to keep an eye on managers. Each additional layer of oversight adds costly agency expenses. (Agency Cost). Because supervision cannot be automated, the Span of Control is tightly constrained to 8–12 people—one manager can at most keep track of this many individuals.

Summary of the traditional framework: Traditional organizations are a function of "human brain cognitive bandwidth." Because humans The capacity to process information is limited, so hierarchy is necessary; because human coordination and communication efficiency is limited, meetings are necessary; because human supervisory attention is limited, a management span is necessary. The pyramid structure is humanity's optimal solution for the "information-scarce era."

5.2 Overview of Changes in the AI Era: Information Abundance and Zero-Cost Coordination

(The Rewrite: Managing Complexity with Intelligence)

AI is not here to improve management; it is here to shake the foundations of management studies. It removes all three constraints mentioned above.

(1) From "information filtering" to "intelligent interpretation"

- Traditional: The core value of middle managers is "passing information up and down"—summarizing complex frontline situations into three points to report to the boss.
- AI: Large models can read all frontline logs, customer recordings, and financial transactions in milliseconds, and directly provide summaries, attributions, early warnings, and decision recommendations. Fracture point: When AI's bandwidth for processing information approaches infinity, "middle layers" are no

longer needed as information relays. The CEO can "penetrate" to the very nerve endings through an AI dashboard.

(2) Coordination no longer relies on "manpower," but on "autonomous execution by agents."

- Traditional: Coordination relies on meetings, emails, and wrangling.
- AI: Agents (AI Agents) take over coordination. After a Sales Agent closes a deal, it automatically triggers the Production Agent to schedule, while notifying the Finance Agent to issue an invoice. Fracture point: Coordination costs shift from exponential growth to near zero. Internal friction in the enterprise disappears, and the organization can operate automatically like software code.

(3) Supervision shifts from "people" to "systems," tearing open the span of control

- Traditional: Relies on KPIs and supervisors' subjective evaluations.
- AI: Relies on full behavioral audit logs (Audit Logs). AI can analyze in real time each employee's/agent's action paths, output quality, and risk behaviors. Fracture point: Supervision becomes an endogenous function of the system. A manager's span of control can leap from 10 people to 100 or even 150.

Three–sentence summary of the transformation:

- Traditional management: Solves the problem of information scarcity (how to obtain information).
- AI management: Solves the problem of information overload (how to interpret information).
- Organizational form: Evolving from "control through hierarchy" to "collaboration through agents."

5.3 In-depth case: Walmart (Walmart)

(Case Study: Managing the Unmanageable Scale)

To show how AI can harness ultra-large-scale complexity, we look at the world's largest company by revenue—Walmart. In a behemoth with 2.1 million employees, improving management efficiency is a matter of life and death. (Data sources: Walmart Annual Report/CNBC/Microsoft Azure Case/MIT Sloan Review)

I. Background: The catastrophe of complexity As the private company with the most employees on Earth, Walmart faces extreme management challenges:

- Decision paralysis: A store manager needs to make over 100 micro-decisions every day (replenishment, scheduling, merchandising).
- Supply chain black box: Tens of thousands of SKUs move around the globe, and logistics managers struggle to sense stockout risks in real time.
- Hierarchical redundancy: It takes a long cycle for information to be transmitted from stores to headquarters. Under traditional logic, maintaining operations at this scale consumes astonishing management costs.

II.AIIntervention:Building a "second-level management structure"2022—2024, Walmart Ma did not solve the problem by adding more managers; instead, she fully introduced AI as an "invisible manager":

- Supply chain brain: AI took over inventory forecasting. It no longer relies on the purchasing managers' experience, but analyzes weather, social media trends, and historical sales data in real time.
- Smart scheduling: AI automatically generates shift schedules for 2.1 million employees based on footfall forecasts, solving the HR department's most headache-inducing coordination challenge.

- Negotiation robots: Walmart has even used Pactum AI robots in procurement to conduct automated long–tail purchasing negotiations with suppliers.

III. Quantified results: A multiplication of management effectiveness

- Replenishment speed: After AI's involvement, replenishment response speed increased by 3 times, and the in–store out–of–stock rate fell by 15%.
- Decision unburdening: The time that store managers and regional managers spend "analyzing data" has decreased by 75%. They are no longer data porters; instead, they have returned to the front lines to manage service and experience.
- Cost optimization: The per–mile cost of logistics transportation has dropped by about 10%, because AI planned routes are superior to those of human dispatchers.

IV. Economic Insights Walmart's case proves the core argument of Chapter 5: AI is the only solution to cope with the complexity of scale. When a company grows to a size beyond the comprehension of the human brain, AI must be introduced as a "second–layer management structure."

- Middle management absorbed: a large number of mid–level managerial tasks responsible for coordination, scheduling, and forecasting are automated by AI.
- Management span expansion: AI enables Walmart to keep expanding its business boundaries without adding management layers. This is not "optimization"; it is a generational leap in management logic.

5.4 Frontline employees' "information overload" and the erosion of managerial authority

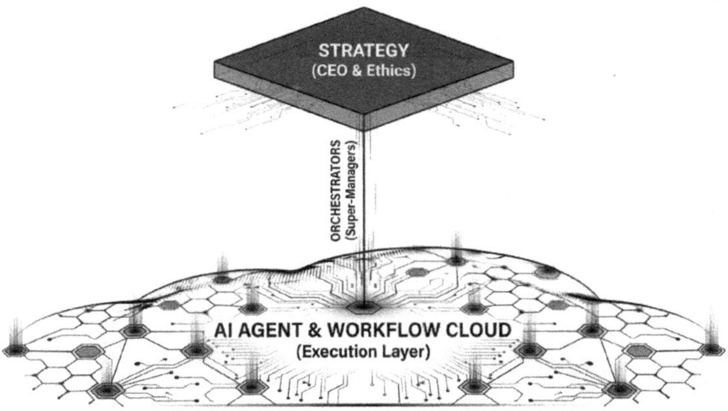

Figure 5-1 | Jason Liu - AI Economics

In the AI era, a frontline sales representative can, through an AI assistant, instantly access market data that is more comprehensive and more real–time than that of a sales director. For the first time, the information advantage has shifted from the top to the front line.

Traditional managerial authority based on "information asymmetry" is crumbling. AI is driving structural changes in the four key management actions:

Information collection (God's–eye view): AI can read the full data from CRM, ERP, finance, and marketing in one pass, allowing managers to see the company's "real–time digital twin" for the first time.

Analysis (insights in seconds): weekly reports and risk analyses that used to take middle managers a week can be completed by AI in 15 seconds.

Decision–making (Scenario Simulation): Managers no longer need to "make decisions on a whim"; instead, they choose AI The best plan yielded after tens of millions of simulations.

Execution (Agent closed loop): AI Agent automatically sends emails, follows up with clients, and drafts contracts. AI is no longer just a thinker, but an executor.

5.5 From a "pyramid" to an "inverted nail" organization

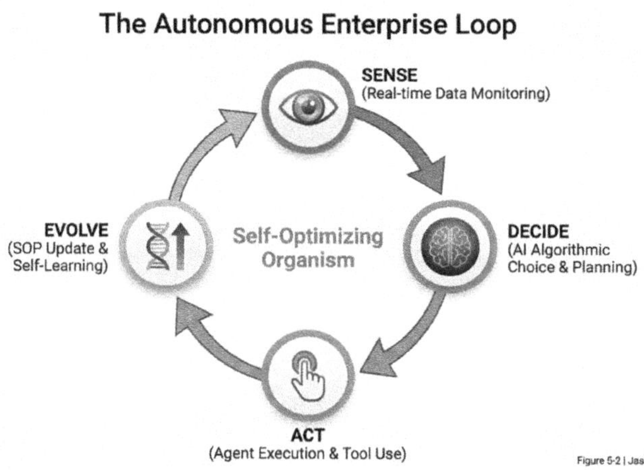

Figure 5-2 | Jason Liu - AI Economics

In the AI era, organizational structures will evolve from the traditional "pyramid" to an "inverted nail" model:

Top layer (a very small group of core decision–makers): They are the "questioners" and "goal setters," responsible for defining the vision and North Star metrics.

Middle layer (sharply compressed): It is expected that within 10 years, middle–management positions will decrease by 60%– 80%. A large number of "overseers" and "mouthpieces" will no longer be needed, replaced by a small group of "AI system maintainers" and "cross–department resource coordinators."

Front line (massively expanded and empowered): A vast number of agile strike units composed of "human experts + AI agents." They are granted substantial autonomy and directly invoke the company's reso Task completed within a closed-loop.

5.6 The essence of management: from "managing people" to "managing AI agents"

The core work of future managers will no longer be meetings, approvals, and making PPTs. Instead, it will shift from "commanding people" to "commanding AI legions." The new roles for future managers include:

AI Orchestrator: Think like a programmer. You are not managing employees, but 30 marketing agents and 20 sales agents. Your core capability is designing workflows and rules for agent collaboration.

Agent Commander: Manage an automatically operating "digital employee ecosystem," handle exceptions, and update rules.

Task Designer: AI does not work on its own. Managers must break down fuzzy business goals into structured task chains that AI can understand.

Human Maximizer: As repetitive work is taken over, the manager's only "people management" duty is to spark team creativity, safeguard mental health, and foster a culture of trust.

5.7 A complete rewrite of management tools: from KPI to AI metric systems

All traditional management tools (KPI, OKR, weekly reports) will be AI-ified:

AI-KPI (agent performance): Managers will no longer focus on headcount, but on "total agent executions," "error rate," "automation ratio," and "AI payback period." AI-OKR: Humans set Objectives (O), and AI automatically decomposes tasks and executes Key Results (KR).

AIPerformance: Employee evaluations no longer focus on workload, but on "AIusage efficiency"—have you leveraged AIto achieve outsized results?

5.8 Case: Morgan Stanley's AI Evals framework

Morgan Stanley has established an internal evaluation framework called "AI Evals" to systematically assess and manage its tens of thousands of AI applications. This framework does not evaluate technical details; it only evaluates their performance, risks, and returns in real business scenarios.

This represents a fundamental shift in management thinking—AI is no longer the domain of the IT department, but a core management tool that every business–unit leader must master.

Chapter summary: Management enters the intelligent era

AI is triggering a profound revolution in management.

By "pushing information downward," it disrupts bureaucracy. Future organizations will take on an "inverted nail" shape: the middle layer disappears, and the frontline gains superpowers. The manager's role evolves from "task overseer" to "AI system designer" + "team psychological coach."

Future enterprises will no longer be hierarchical organizations, but an "agent operating system" driven by human intent.

Actionable Takeaways (Actionable Takeaways)

For managers:

Abandon "control":

You must accept a fact: you are no longer the smartest person on the team. Your job is not to provide the answers, but to ask good questions and to provide resources and authority to the team (including the AI team).

Learn to "think like AI":

Start learning to draw flowcharts, learn data analysis, and learn how to turn a vague objective Break it down into clear steps. You need to have a "systems engineer" mindset.

Invest in "soft skills":

When hard skills can be replaced by AI, soft skills (listening, empathy, nonviolent communication) become your strongest armor. These distinctly "human" abilities will be your irreplaceable value as a human manager.

Chapter 6

AIReshapes Industry Structure: Winner-Takes-All or Long-Tail Rise?

Academic positioning of this chapter: from Industrial Organization theory (IO) to the intelligent bimodal structure

Why do some industries have only one giant, while others are filled with countless small players? Before we dive into how AI will restructure industries, we need to draw on industrial organization theory.

Through the lens of Industrial Organization, understand the underlying forces that determine industry structure.

I. The Foundations of Traditional IO Theory

Cost Structure: The ratio of fixed costs to marginal costs, which determines an industry's potential for concentration.

Barriers to Entry: The height of the moat determines the durability of profits.

Network Effects: Determines the winner–takes–all nature of platform companies.

II. Revisions to traditional assumptions (the rupture brought by AI)

Amendment 1: Cost polarization. AI simultaneously drives fixed costs (compute threshold) sharply higher and pushes marginal costs (service threshold) sharply lower, making the middle form unsustainable.

Amendment 2: Coordination mechanism. Market coordination shifts from "price signals" to "algorithmic matching," reshaping supply–demand relationships.

Amendment 3: Structural change. Industries shift from a normal distribution (olive–shaped) to a bimodal distribution (dumbbell–shaped).

III. Forward-Looking Case: Mercado Libre's dumbbell-shaped reconstruction

To validate the formation of a "bimodal structure," we analyze the Latin American e–commerce giant Mercado Libre.

On one hand, it uses AI to optimize its massive logistics network (strengthening head–tier moats); on the other, it provides AI generation tools to millions of micro and small merchants (empowering long–tail prosperity). This case clearly shows how middle–layer traders are squeezed out, while a dumbbell–shaped ecosystem of "giants + super individuals" becomes established.

6.0 Introduction: AI's impact on industries is not "optimization," but "reconstruction."

Many entrepreneurs mistakenly believe AI is just an "efficiency tool" like CRM or ERP, used to optimize the existing industry landscape. This is an extremely dangerous misjudgment.

AI changes the industry's supply structure (who can produce), cost structure (marginal costs approach zero), competitive structure (moats shift), and organizational structure. In this chapter, we will explore the ultimate form of future industry evolution—the "Barbell Structure."

Imagine a dumbbell:

On one end are a very few super giants: they command compute and data, so powerful they have no peers. On the other end are countless highly agile super individuals: they arm themselves to the teeth with AI, and thrive.

In the middle lies the most dangerous "valley of death": mid-sized companies that lack the scale of giants and the flexibility of individuals will face an unprecedented "hollowing out" crisis.

6.1 Traditional Industrial Organization (IO) framework

(Theoretical Foundations of Industrial Organization)

The core question studied in Industrial Organization (IO) is: Why do industries look the way they do? Why are there only two companies in aircraft manufacturing, while there are countless firms in food service?

All industrial structures are jointly determined by the following four core variables:

(1) Cost Structure: The Physical Laws of an Industry

The foundation of traditional IO is the "cost structure," especially the interplay between two key concepts:

Fixed Cost (FC): The "ticket" you must pay to enter an industry, such as building factories and developing systems.

Marginal Cost (MC): The additional cost to serve one more customer.

IO First Law: High fixed costs + low marginal costs = natural monopoly / oligopolistic tendency.

Telecommunications: Laying fiber-optic cables (FC) is extremely expensive, while connecting a new user (MC) is very cheap → oligopolistic monopoly.

Consulting: Little need for equipment (low FC), but each additional client requires human time (high MC) → hard to monopolize, highly fragmented.

(2) Barriers to Entry: The Depth of the Moat

Whether competition in an industry is intense depends on barriers to entry (Barriers to Entry).

Structural barriers: economies of scale, absolute cost advantages (e.g., controlling a mine). Strategic barriers: patent walls, exclusive agreements, brand loyalty.

The higher the barriers, the longer incumbent firms can sustain excess profits; the lower the barriers, the closer the industry moves toward perfect competition, with profits tending toward zero.

(3) Four types of market structures

Based on the above variables, traditional economics divides all industries into four categories:

Perfect competition: no barriers, homogeneous products (e.g., agricultural products).

Monopolistic competition: low barriers, differentiated products (e.g., apparel, dining).

Oligopoly: high barriers, strategic interaction among a few giants (e.g., automobiles, banking).

Monopoly: extremely high barriers, exclusive operation (e.g., the power grid).

(4) Economies of scale and network effects

These are the two "natural laws" that determine the landscape of the tech industry:

Economies of scale: the larger the production scale, the lower the unit cost. This is the logic of the industrial era.

Network effects: the more users there are, the greater the value to each user. This is the logic of the internet era (e.g., WeChat, Uber).

These two effects are the strongest forces driving industries to concentrate at the top.

(5) Structure–Conduct–Performance (SCP) paradigm

Traditional IO holds that industries follow the SCP logic: Structure determines conduct (Conduct), and conduct determines performance (Performance). Industry structure is typically stable unless a major technological shock occurs.

AI is precisely such a once–in–a–century shock.

6.2 Overview of changes in the AI era: the industry's "fracture triangle"

(The Shift: The Dumbbell Structure)

With the arrival of AI, industry structure for the first time is tearing simultaneously toward two extremes: stronger at the top, stronger in the long tail, and a collapse in the middle.

(1) Fixed costs surge → sky-high barriers for the leaders

AI's "entry ticket"—ten–thousand–card GPU clusters, trillion–scale training data, and top–tier scientist teams—is extraordinarily expensive.

This leads the Foundation Model layer and the infrastructure layer to possess inherently high natural–monopoly attributes. Small and medium–sized enterprises have virtually no room to survive at this layer.

(2) Marginal costs go to zero → an explosion among long-tail individuals

AI has endowed individuals with "small–team–level" productivity. The marginal cost of copywriting, design, coding, and preliminary legal review is approaching zero.

This means Super–Individuals and micro–enterprises now possess unprecedented competitiveness. They are extremely agile and operate at very low cost.

(3) Intelligence scale effects (Scaling Laws) → winner-takes-all acceleration

Traditional network effects focus only on "number of users." In the AI era, a "data flywheel" has emerged:

this self-reinforcing loop makes the moats of leading companies (such as OpenAI and Google) even deeper than in the internet era.

(4) Coordination mechanism: from "prices" to "algorithms"

Traditional: prices coordinate supply and demand.

AI: algorithms (Algorithms) directly coordinate supply and demand. Recommendation systems not only match demand but even create demand. Industry competition has escalated from "price wars" to "algorithm-efficiency wars."

(5) Result: dumbbell structure (Dumbbell Structure)

Head: giants controlling compute and data.

Long tail: Super-Individuals who command niche scenarios and trust.

Middle: Medium-sized enterprises that have neither economies of scale nor flexibility (Middle Market) are facing structural extinction.

6.3 In-depth Case: Mercado Libre (Meli)

(Case Study: AI Reshaping the Latin American Commerce Ecosystem)

To validate the formation of a "barbell-shaped structure," we turn to Latin America's largest e-commerce and fintech giant—Mercado Libre.

(Data sources: Mercado Libre Annual Report / Microsoft Azure / MIT Tech Review)

I. Background: The Aggregation Challenge in a Fragmented Market

The Latin American market is vast in geography, with weak logistics infrastructure and low financial inclusion. Traditional theory suggests that such a market is unlikely to form an efficient unified platform and is more likely to see a coexistence of numerous regional mid–sized companies.

But Mercado Libre used AI to rewrite this script.

II. AI Intervention: Extreme Empowerment at Both Ends

Meli's AI strategy precisely targets the "middle layer" while empowering both the "head" and the "long tail."

Empowering the long tail (supply side): Meli launched a seller assistant based on GenAI. Small merchants only need to upload a photo, and AI automatically generates multilingual product titles, descriptions, and attributes

It can even auto–optimize ad placement by tweaking parameters, giving a small artisan from rural Brazil operational capabilities on par with major brands.

Strengthening the head (platform side): Meli leveraged AI to reconstruct its entire logistics network (Mercado Envíos). Algorithms plan thousands of routes in real time and forecast parcel volumes for each neighborhood. On the risk control side, AI models process hundreds of millions of transactions within milliseconds, driving fraud loss rates down to the lowest in the industry.

III. Quantitative results: the disappearance of the middle layer

Operational efficiency: AI delivers a 100x improvement in operational efficiency (official tech blog).

Market structure: Latin America's e–commerce market is rapidly consolidating around Meli, squeezing out many medium–sized traders and logistics agents that previously survived on "information asymmetry."

Long–tail prosperity: Millions of micro and small merchants relying on AI tools are active on the platform, forming Meli's vast ecosystem base.

IV. Economic insights

The case of Mercado Libre perfectly illustrates this chapter's core logic: AI amplifies the head, amplifies the long tail, and compresses the middle.

The platform's algorithms, compute power, and models constitute insurmountable barriers (making the head even stronger).

AI toolchains reduce individual merchants' marginal costs to zero (with an even stronger long–tail effect).

Industry structure is no longer a pyramid; it has evolved into a bimodal pattern in the intelligent era.

6.4 How does technology determine industry structure? AI breaks traditional models

Over the past 300 years, each technological revolution has reshaped industry structures, but in different directions:

Electrification (tilted toward scale): Huge fixed costs led to the rise of large enterprises (e.g., General Electric).

Internet (tilted toward platforms): Network effects led to winner–takes–all (e.g., Google). But in the AI era, three forces have emerged that are entirely different from the traditional industrial age; they act like three surgical scalpels, performing bidirectional cuts across industries:

Intelligent scale effects: The stronger the compute, the higher the intelligence (favoring giants).

Intelligent agent network effects: The more Agents, the stronger the collaboration (favoring ecosystems).

Data flywheel effects: More users \rightarrow more data \rightarrow more accurate models \rightarrow more users (favoring first movers).

AI is the first technology in human history to shape industry structure in both directions: it makes the strong stronger, and it also makes the weak stronger.

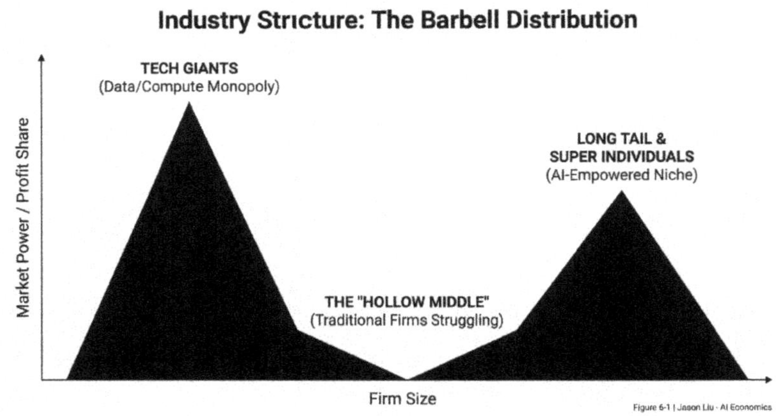

6.5 Why will AI make leading enterprises even stronger? (Winner-Takes-Most)

In search, e–commerce, social networks, and foundational large models, we will see a "winner–takes–all" landscape that is even more cutthroat than in the internet era.

1. Scaling Law and inference scaling effects

When model parameters reach the trillion level, "emergent capabilities" appear. Small models are not just less intelligent—they fundamentally "don't understand human language." This causes users to irreversibly converge on the smartest top–tier models. Only a handful of companies can build large models.

2. Compute and infrastructure barriers (High Capex Barrier)

Training a frontier model requires tens of thousands of H100 GPUs and hundreds of millions of dollars in power infrastructure. Fewer than 8 tech giants worldwide (such as Microsoft/OpenAI, Google, Meta, Amazon) have this ticket to entry. Small and medium–sized enterprises simply cannot compete at the "base" layer.

3. Risk alert: the backlash of the data flywheel (Model Collapse)

Although leading enterprises possess data hegemony, they face a fatal "genetic defect" risk—model collapse (Model Collapse). If a future GPT–6 is trained on internet data generated by GPT–5, it will be akin to inbreeding, and model quality will degrade.

Commercial value: Therefore, "real high–quality human data" (letters, medical records, transaction records not contaminated by AI) will become a strategic resource more precious than gold.

6.6 Why does AI simultaneously enable a long-tail boom? (Tail Explosion)

This is the most favorable news for ordinary people. AI is triggering a "long–tail detonation."

1. Startup Cost Collapse (Startup Cost Collapse)

In the past, the threshold for starting a business was "5 people, 5 million, 18 months." Now, AI enables 1 person to handle product, marketing, customer service, and finance. The startup threshold has become "1 person, 50,000, 1 month."

Productivity revolution for micro–enterprises: In the past, opening an advertising agency required at least 10 people—copywriters, designers, and planners. Now, "you + AI" = a 10–person team.

2. Tool democratization and skill amplification (Skill Amplification)

An entrepreneur in a small town can use the exact same GPT–4o model as a Fortune 500 CEO. The technology gap has been leveled. AI helps programmers write better code and turns agents into super agents.

3. The rise of super individuals (Super Individuals)

Over the next 5 years, we will see lawyers, real estate agents, and designers earning millions or even tens of millions annually, with no employees—only a vast "digital workforce."

6.7 Industry structure shifts to a "bi-modal distribution" with a hollowed-out middle

The industrial structure will evolve into: super–monopolies at the top + a super–prosperous long tail, rather than the past "olive–shaped" structure with a bulging middle.

AI–driven restructuring of industry is intensifying the trend toward a "bi–modal distribution."

Hollowing Out of the Middle (Hollowing Out of the Middle):

The Report on the Development of Small and Medium–sized Enterprises (2025) reveals a survival crisis for a vast number of SMEs amid the digital wave. Lacking sufficient data accumulation, high–end AI talent, and sustained compute investment capacity, firms with 50–500 employees engaged in standardized services (such as mediocre translation companies, outsourced customer service firms, and general design institutes) can neither match the efficiency of giants nor compete with individuals' flexibility and low prices, facing the risk of being disrupted from a higher dimension.

New-quality champions (rise of the peaks):

On the other hand, as shown by KPMG's analysis of new–quality leaders in high–end equipment in the Yangtze River Delta, a group of industry champions mastering "new–quality productivity" is emerging. These companies con

tinue to build extremely high technical moats and ecosystem barriers by deeply integrating AI, big data, and advanced manufacturing technologies, becoming the new dominant players at the "peaks" of their industries.

2025 data corroboration: the "Matthew Effect" in brand value

According to the Global 500 Most Valuable Brands Report (2025), AI has intensified the "Matthew Effect" in the brand world. Tech giants that have successfully integrated AI into their products, services, and marketing systems have achieved brand value growth that significantly surpasses the average level.

6.8 Which industries will end up on which side? Assessment model

We propose a simple yet highly practical decision model (Class A vs Class B):

Class A: Industries prone to "head concentration" (the stronger AI becomes, the more monopolistic)

Characteristics: massive data, economies of scale, algorithm-driven, high capital investment.

Domains: general search, e-commerce platforms, standardized financial services, foundational content platforms, autonomous driving, chips.

Logic: prioritizes efficiency and scale; only giants survive.

Class B: Industries prone to a "long tail" (the stronger AI becomes, the more fragmented)

Characteristics: localized services, high-trust relationships, irreplaceable emotion, creativity/expression matter.

Domains: education and consulting (tutoring tailored to specific children), creator economy (internet influencers/writers), healthcare and caregiving (work requiring a handshake and reassurance), professional services (lawyers/accountants).

Logic: AI cannot replace human relationships; AI amplifies the capabilities of ordinary individuals.

Class C: Hybrid industries (real estate as a special case)

Real estate is a typical industry where the head and the long tail are integrated, which directly validates your company's strategy:

Head effect: Portal platforms (such as Zillow, Beike) leverage data to monopolize traffic.

Long–tail effect: The transaction itself requires extremely high trust; AI cannot replace the person who takes you to view properties and gives you confidence.

Conclusion: The "AI full–stack real estate company" (Longmei Real Estate) you are building is the dominant model for the next 10 years: head platforms + AI–strong enterprises + a large number of AI–augmented small agents.

6.9 The particularity of China's industry structure

According to CNNIC (2025) data, China exhibits a distinctive "application–driven" structure. AI has very high penetration in content creation (45.8%), education (41.4%), and customer service (38%).

Chinese companies are exceptionally adept at landing AI in concrete scenarios (such as digital humans for e–commerce livestreaming), which forms the unique competitiveness of China's AI industry—although the underlying models may not be the strongest, the ability to generate revenue and monetize is extremely strong.

6.10 North America vs. Asia: industry structure differences

North America: Innovation–driven. Led by OpenAI and Google, with a complete chip (Nvidia) and operating system ecosystem.

Asia: Scenario–driven. Lightweight models (SmallLLMs) are highly prevalent on mobile phones and IoT devices.

Europe: Governance–driven. Constrained by GDPR and the AI Act, with a primary focus on explainable

AI and industrial AI.

Chapter Summary

Industry structure is shifting from a "pyramid" to a "barbell."

AI makes the strong stronger (winner–takes–all in industries reliant on scale, data, and capital), while also making the weak stronger (a long–tail boom in industries reliant on relationships, services, and human factors).

The middle tier of companies will be ruthlessly eliminated. You either become a giant that controls core compute power, or a super individual that commands core customer trust. Do not remain stuck in the mediocre middle.

Actionable Takeaways (Actionable Takeaways)

For entrepreneurs:

Positioning self-assessment (a life-or-death question):

Where is your company positioned on the barbell? If you're in the middle (for example, an ordinary

100–person translation firm), you must act immediately: either merge and scale up to become a leader, or break apart and downsize into a flexible network of experts.

Build a private "data well" (moat):

Do not try to compete with the giants on general–purpose large models. Go collect those in your industry

that Google can't find (such as specific maintenance logs, customers' complaint recordings), clean them thoroughly—this will be your only moat in the future.

Startup advice (control scale):

If you are starting a business now, set a rule: before revenue exceeds 10,000,000, do not have more than 5 full–time employees. If something can be solved by an AI Agent or SaaS, do not hire.

Chapter 7

AI and Economic Growth: From the Solow Model to the "Compute GDP" Model

Academic positioning of this chapter: From Exogenous Growth Theory to a Compute–Driven Endogenous Model (Compute–Driven Endogenous Model)

Why do some countries fall into the middle–income trap, while others keep breaking through the growth ceiling?

When "intelligence" itself becomes a factor that can be industrially produced like electricity,

where is the upper limit of GDP growth?

Before we delve into how AI reshapes growth, we need to use the lens of macroeconomic growth theory to understand the dynamics behind national wealth creation.

I. The foundations of traditional growth theory

Solow Growth Model: This is the crown jewel of growth theory. It posits that economic growth mainly comes from capital accumulation, increases in labor, and technological progress.

Diminishing Returns to Capital: Simply piling up machines (capital deepening) cannot sustain long–term growth. When capital per capita reaches a certain level, the incremental output from each additional machine becomes smaller and smaller, and the economy ultimately settles at a "steady state."

Solow Residual: Solow found that after deducting the contributions of capital and labor, the remaining unexplained portion of growth is "Total Factor Productivity (TFP)." In traditional models, TFP is treated as exogenous "technological progress," like "a pie falling from the sky," which economists cannot explain how it arises.

II. Revisions to traditional assumptions (the rupture brought by AI)

Amendment 1: Endogenizing technology. AI opens the black box of the Solow residual. Technological progress is no longer random luck; it becomes a function of inputs in Compute, Data, and Models. As long as investment in compute increases, predictable technological progress can be achieved. Growth becomes a controllable engineering problem.

Amendment 2: Increasing returns to scale. Intelligent capital (models) exhibits strong network effects and self–iteration capabilities (Scaling Laws). The larger the inputs, the stronger the model; marginal returns may rise rather than fall, breaking the fate of traditional growth convergence.

Amendment 3: Energy constraints. AI tightly binds growth in the virtual world to energy in the physical world. In future growth formulas, Electricity (Energy) will become a harder constraint than capital.

III. Forward-looking Case: NVIDIA's Growth Engine

To validate "compute is growth," we analyze the chip giant NVIDIA.

It is not just a company that sells graphics cards; it is a new "physical engine" of global economic growth. From 2020 to 2024, the explosive growth of NVIDIA's data center business essentially reflects humanity's feverish conversion of "capital" into "intelligent technology" (TFP).

NVIDIA's GPU reserves are becoming a core metric for gauging a country's or a company's potential GDP growth rate.

7.0 Introduction: The stalled growth engine and the only lifeline

If you are still using traditional GDP growth logic to view the future, you may be misled.

Macroscopic backdrop: the growth engine stalls

To understand countries' strategic anxiety about AI, we must place it in the broader macroeconomic context. "Asian Financial Watch (2025)" points out that the world's traditional engines of economic growth (such as real estate, demographic dividends, and export–led development) are gradually stalling. Against this backdrop, the productivity revolution sparked by AI has become almost the only hope to break zero–sum competition and restart the growth cycle.

The AI revolution of 2023–2025 shows that traditional growth models have failed. AI has introduced an entirely new growth paradigm: compounding growth driven by intelligent capital. We are entering an era of Compute GDP.

7.1 Traditional economic growth theory: the Solow model's black box

(The Black Box of Growth: Solow Model)

The core mission of macroeconomics is to explain growth. Why are some countries rich and others poor? Why do some periods grow rapidly (such as the 1990s), while others fall into stagnation? To answer this question, Nobel laureate Robert Solow (Robert Solow) proposed the famous Solow growth model. It has been the theoretical cornerstone of all growth policies over the past 70 years.

(1) The three sources of growth

The Solow model holds that an economy's output (Y) is determined by three factors:

1. Labor (L): How many people are working.
2. Capital (K): How much machinery and equipment there is.
3. Technology (A): How high production efficiency is.

The formula is still the familiar production function, but in growth theory, what we look at is dynamic change:

(2) The fate of capital accumulation: diminishing marginal returns

Can we rely on frenzied factory building (increasing K) to sustain long-term growth? No. One of the core insights of the Solow model is diminishing marginal returns to capital. When a country moves from poverty to moderate prosperity, building roads and factories is highly effective; but when the capital stock is already high (as in developed countries), adding yet another highway has a negligible effect on GDP. Therefore, mere capital accumulation cannot achieve sustained long-term growth, and the economy will ultimately settle into a "steady state (Steady State)."

(3) The hard constraint of labor: population determinism

Can we rely on a manpower strategy (increasing L)? It's difficult. Labor supply is constrained by the natural population growth rate. In an aging society, L can even be negative. Growth driven by the demographic dividend is unsustainable.

(4) Total Factor Productivity (TFP): The mysterious "Solow residual"

Since capital faces diminishing marginal returns and population growth can stagnate, why has human society still managed to keep growing for two centuries? There is only one answer: technological progress (A). In economics, this is called Total Factor Productivity (TFP).

- Definition: The portion of output growth that remains after subtracting the contributions of capital and labor inputs.

- Essence: It represents all the factors—such as innovation, managerial efficiency, and institutional optimization—that enable "the same inputs to produce more."

(5) Biggest flaw: Technology is "exogenous"

Although the Solow model identifies technology (A) as the sole source of long–run growth, it has a fatal theoretical flaw: it assumes technological progress is an exogenous variable (Exogenous). This means that in traditional models, technology is like "manna from heaven." Economists can observe it but cannot explain why it occurs, nor can they control it through mechanisms within the model. The awkward state of growth theory: we know growth depends entirely on technology, yet we know nothing about how technology arises. This is called the "black box" of growth theory.

7.2 Overview of changes in the AI era: Endogenizing technology and the compute engine

(The Rewrite: Endogenous Growth via Compute)

The impact of AI on economic growth is far more than mere "efficiency gains." It shakes the three deepest foundations of the traditional growth model and, for the first time in 70 years, opens that sealed "black box."

(1) TechnologyAFrom "Black Box" to "Engineering"

- Traditional: A is random and exogenous.
- AI: A has become an endogenous variable that can be precisely manufactured. For the first time, we have found that as long as we increase compute supply, feed in more data, and iterate model architectures, the technology level (A) will improve along a predictable curve (Scaling Laws). Technological progress has become an investable, stackable industrial good.

(2) Qualitative shift in capital K: Compute equals growth

- Traditional: Capital is physical (machines) and is governed by the law of diminishing marginal returns.
- AI: Capital has become an "intelligent compute network." Due to Scaling Laws, within a certain range, the more compute invested, the stronger the model, the broader the applications, and returns may even become increasing. Capital K and technology A have fused: investing in compute (K) is directly purchasing technological progress (A).

(3) The decoupling of labor L: infinite supply

- Traditional: L is constrained by population.
- AI: L_{ext{eff}}=L_{ext{human}}+\lambda\cdot L
- AI: Intelligent agents (Agents) serve as digital labor, and their supply is limited only by energy and chips. Economic growth is no longer locked in by low fertility rates.

(4) The measurability of TFP

- Traditional: TFP is an "unaccountable residual."
- AI: The sources of TFP become clearly visible—compute density, data quality, and model parameter count. Countries can directly intervene in these variables through policy to drive TFP.

(5) Core conclusion: From resource-driven to intelligence-driven, for the first time in history, GDP growth rate shows a strong positive correlation with GPU compute growth rate. The physical engine of economic growth has shifted from burning oil to burning compute.

7.3 In-depth case: NVIDIA

(Case Study: The Physical Engine of Global Growth)

To substantiate the claim that "compute equals growth," we must study NVIDIA. It is not merely a $3 trillion chip company; it is the physical embodiment of the global economic growth function in the AI era. (Data sources: NVIDIA Annual Report/Financial Times/MIT Tech Review)

I. Background: From "graphics card vendor" to "growth engine." In traditional economic classifications, NVIDIA is merely a link in high-end manufacturing, producing capital goods for gaming. But in the AI era, its role has undergone a qualitative change: it has become the sole upstream of global technological progress (A).

- Any country that wants to grow GDP (raise A) must purchase H100/B200GPU.
- Any enterprise that wants to improve TFP must connect to compute clouds based on the NVIDIA architecture.

II. AI intervention: rewriting the logic of growth. NVIDIA's breakout was not the result of a semiconductor cycle, but the result of "technology endogenization."

- Data center revenue surge: From 2020 to 2024, its data center business revenue grew by more than 400%. This indicates that humanity is feverishly converting "capital" into "intelligent technology."
- Full-stack ecosystem: NVIDIA doesn't just sell hardware (K); it sells productivity (A) through CUDA and the AIEnterprise software stack, directly delivering productivity (A).

III. Quantitative results: the coupling of compute and the economy

- Marginal cost break: NVIDIA's GPUs have reduced the cost of training large models by a factor of 1,000,000 every 10 years (Huang's Law). This technological deflation directly fuels the explosion of downstream applications.
- Return on capital: Tech giants (Microsoft, Meta, Google) invest tens of billions of dollars annually to purchase NVIDIA chips. In traditional terms, this looks like "insane capital expenditure," but in the AI growth model, it is "stockpiling future growth rates."

IV. Economic insights. NVIDIA' s case proves the core logic of this chapter: A = f (Compute).

- Technology is no longer exogenous: it is built by stacking GPU computing power.
- Growth can be bought: as long as there is sufficient energy and chips, an economy can break through the traditional Production Possibility Frontier (PPF). NVIDIA is the "steam engine manufacturing bureau" of the intelligence era, defining the upper bound of global economic growth speed.

7.4 Why can't traditional growth models explain AI?

Comparison of Traditional vs. AI-Era GDP Composition

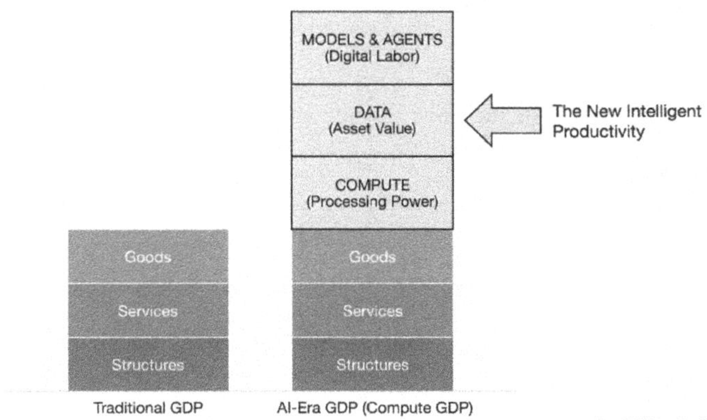

Figure 7-1 | Jason Liu - AI Economics

Over the past 70 years, the primary model used worldwide has been the Solow Growth Model. Its core assumptions are: diminishing marginal returns to capital accumulation, labor growth constrained by population, and technology being exogenous (a gift from God).

But AI completely breaks these three premises:

Diminishing marginal returns to capital → reversed by AI. The more compute, the stronger the models, exhibiting increasing returns.

Labor cannot expand infinitely → broken by AI's limitless replication. The labor supply (L) is no longer constrained by the number of young people, but by the number of GPUs.

Technology is exogenous → broken by AI's endogenization. Technology is no longer a variable we can only pray will happen; it has become a controllable variable "endogenously" determined by compute, data, and models.

As long as you pour money into buying compute, intelligence will improve and productivity will grow. This is the biggest theoretical upgrade in macroeconomics in 70 years.

7.5 Inference Cost Curve shows a break

This is the most important economics chart of this chapter: the Inference Cost Curve.

The most important economic variable in the AI era is not the price of GPUs, but the cost per unit of intelligent inference (Inference). In recent years, this cost has fallen by two orders of magnitude. This means that "thinking" has become extremely cheap.

When "thinking" becomes cheap, we can add intelligent judgment to any tiny step (such as adjusting the air–conditioner temperature or planning parcel delivery routes), thereby unlocking massive efficiency gains.

7.6 New economic growth framework: AI as an endogenous growth engine

AI's growth mechanism operates through three channels:

Channel One: AI enhances effective labor (Labor Augmentation)

AI has effectively expanded the "labor tray" without limit. The supply curve of AI labor is perfectly elastic (Perfectly Elastic); as long as there is power, it can replicate indefinitely. Firms can scale capacity at unprecedented speed without facing "hiring bottlenecks."

Channel Two: AI improves capital efficiency (Capital Efficiency)

AI automatically optimizes investment decisions, reduces supply chain waste, and lowers risk, raising the marginal product of capital.

Channel Three: AI boosts TFP (Total Factor Productivity)

AI is not just fast at getting things done; it also enables better resource allocation.

Example: An AI-dispatched power grid can carry 20% more load than a human-dispatched grid. This additional 20% is a pure improvement in TFP.

7.7 Intelligence-augmented production functions and energy constraints

We construct a growth equation for the AI era (the GAIA hypothesis):

In this formula, output no longer depends on population, but on AI's IQ (AIIQ) and compute投入.

The hard constraint of energy (E)

Silicon-based labor doesn't eat bread, but it consumes electricity. The physical essence of compute is energy conversion. Therefore, only when energy costs are sufficiently low can the labor of intelligent agents truly scale without bound. The great-power game of the future is not only a chip war, but also an energy war (especially over controlled nuclear fusion and clean electricity).

7.8 Compute GDP: A new model for understanding GDP in the AI era

Future GDP accounting must be reformed. I believe that in the AI era, GDP should include a fourth major sector: the intelligent generation services industry.

To assess a city's economic potential, don't just look at how many office buildings it has; look at how many PFLOPS (compute units) it possesses and how efficiently that compute is utilized.

7.8 AI will reshape the global economic landscape: compute-rich countriesvscompute-poor countries

The past global stratification was “developedvsdeveloping.”In the AIera, it will become:

Countries with computevscountries without compute

Countries with datavscountries without data

Whoever controls low–cost compute and energy holds the key to growth. This will determine future GDP growth rates, industrial competitiveness, and national security.

7.10 Where are the limits to AI's growth?

AIdrives growth, but it is also constrained by five major bottlenecks:Compute bottleneck:GPU/TPUsupply shortages.Energy bottleneck:AIenergy consumption is surging.

Data bottleneck:High–quality human data is running out, requiring synthetic data (Synthetic Data).

Governance bottleneck:AIsafety and regulation.

Inequality bottleneck: Growth may come with greater polarization.

Chapter Summary

For the first time, economic growth is determined by “intelligent capability.”

AI is the single strongest driver of global economic growth from 2025 to 2045. We must shift from the Solow model to an AI growth model and embrace a compute–driven future.

Actionable Takeaways (Actionable Takeaways)

For investors and decision–makers:

Investment perspective (hard tech):

Focus resolutely on companies that provide the "shovels" and the "water."

"Shovels": chip manufacturing, advanced packaging, optical modules.

"Water": power infrastructure, transformers, thermal management technologies, green–energy data centers.

Corporate decision-making (TCO mindset):

When calculating your "AI employee cost," don't just look at the per–call price of the API; assess the total cost of ownership (TCO) across the full lifecycle, including energy consumption, operations and maintenance, and retraining costs stemming from model obsolescence.

Policy recommendations:

If you are a policymaker, make "reducing the reasoning cost for the whole society" your top priority for boosting GDP. Only when the cost of reasoning is low will small and medium–sized enterprises be able to afford AI, and only then can the economy prosper.

Chapter 8

AI and Inflation: The Two-Way Forces of Technological Deflation and Asset Inflation

Academic positioning of this chapter: From the Quantity Theory of Money to the Dual–Track Intelligent Inflation Model

When "intelligence" becomes as cheap as air and "computing power" becomes as precious as gold, can the traditional Consumer Price Index (CPI) still reflect the real world?

Is the future a deflationary winter, or an inflationary blaze?

Before we enter the discussion of "intelligent inflation," we need to use the lens of macro monetary theory to understand the classical mechanics behind price fluctuations.

I. The cornerstone of traditional inflation theory

Demand–Pull: The core view of Keynesianism—"too much money chasing too few goods." When aggregate demand exceeds aggregate supply, prices rise.

Cost–Push: The supply–side logic. Increases in raw materials (such as oil) or wages lead to higher production costs, forcing firms to raise prices. This often results in the dreaded "wage–price spiral."

price–wage spiral.

Monetary phenomenon (Monetary Phenomenon): Friedman's assertion—"Inflation is always and everywhere a monetary phenomenon." The central bank's pace of money creation determines the long–term price level.

II. Revisions to traditional assumptions (the rupture brought by AI)

Amendment 1: Intelligence Deflation. AI drives the marginal cost of high–cognition services (law, programming, translation) toward zero. This creates a powerful downward pull on service–sector prices—an unforeseen "cognitive oversupply" in traditional models.

Amendment 2: Asset Inflation. The "new oil" required to produce intelligence

(GPUs, clean electricity, data) has extremely low supply elasticity, while demand is exploding exponentially. This exerts upward pressure on underlying hard–asset prices.

Amendment 3: Structural tearing (K–Shaped Split). Unlike the broad–based rises or falls of traditional inflation, the AI era exhibits a K–shaped pattern of "soft–service deflation + hard–asset inflation," causing conventional CPI indicators to be seriously distorted.

III. Forward-looking case: AWS's dual-track pricing

To validate this "split," we analyze AWS (Amazon Web Services), the compute powerhouse.

On one hand, AWS has reduced unit prices for AI inference services by 70%–90% over five years through technological progress (output deflation); on the other hand, its underlying costs for data center construction, power procurement, and GPU hardware have surged sharply (input inflation).

AWS is a microcosm of the global compute pricing system, perfectly illustrating how deflation and inflation can contend within the same entity.

8.0 Introduction: AI's impact on inflation is a "two-way force."

Everyone is asking: Will AI make things cheaper or more expensive?

The answer is: extremely cheap, and at the same time, extremely expensive.

AI is the first time in human history to simultaneously bring about: drastic technological deflation (services and software become cheaper) and drastic asset inflation (computing power, electricity, and core data become more expensive). This is an unprecedented "schizophrenic" inflation structure.

8.1 Traditional inflation theory framework: the classical mechanics of prices

(The Mechanics of Price: Traditional Inflation Theory)

Inflation is one of the oldest and most sensitive issues in macroeconomics. It answers a simple question that concerns everyone's wallet: Why do things get more expensive? Traditional economics explains inflation primarily on the basis of the following three pillars:

(1) Demand-Pull Inflation

This is the core view of Keynesianism: "too much money chasing too few goods."

- Mechanism: When consumer confidence surges, corporate investment spikes, or the government floods the economy with money, the aggregate demand curve shifts to the right. If capacity (supply) cannot expand quickly enough, prices will be "pulled" up by buyers.
- Typical scenarios: the post–World War II boom in the United States; periods of overheated real estate markets.

(2) Cost-Push Inflation

This is a supply–side nightmare. Even if nobody wants to buy more, if production costs rise, prices have to go up.

- Mechanism: Increases in the prices of raw materials (oil), wages, or imported goods lead to enterpri The industry's production costs increase, and the aggregate supply curve shifts to the left.
- Typical scenarios: the oil crisis of the 1970s and the global supply chain disruptions after the COVID–19 pandemic. These are often accompanied by the most alarming "wage–price spiral": prices rise o workers demand higher wages o corporate costs increase o prices continue to rise.

(3) Monetary Theory: Friedman's Assertion

Nobel laureate Milton Friedman once said: "Inflation is, everywhere and always, a monetary phenomenon."

- Core logic: If the central bank prints money faster than the economy produces goods, the currency will depreciate.
- Points of focus: M2 (broad money supply), interest rates, and the required reserve ratio. In this school's view, the only button for controlling inflation is in the hands of the central bank.

(4) Structural Inflation and Expectations

- Structural inflation: long–term high prices (such as in healthcare and education) caused by market monopolies, regulatory constraints, or imbalances in the industrial structure. This is often institutional rather than cyclical.
- Expectations theory: The most dangerous variable in inflation is "public sentiment." If the general public expects prices to be higher next year, they will rush to buy now, thereby self–fulfilling inflation.

(5) Measuring Stick: The Limitations of CPI

To measure inflation, we invented the CPI (Consumer Price Index). It is a weighted average of a basket of goods including food, housing, transportation, and more. But the CPI has three inherent flaws that are magnified in the AI era:

1. Failure to capture quality improvements: today's iPhone is a hundred times more powerful than it was 10 years ago, but the CPI only records that its price has increased by 20%.

2. Ignores asset prices: even when housing prices and stock indices soar, the CPI may barely move.

3. Slow to reflect tech–driven deflation: free digital services (such as search and navigation) cannot be included in the CPI.

Summary of the traditional framework: From a traditional perspective, prices are jointly determined by the supply–demand gap, production costs, the money supply, and public expectations. This logic still holds in the real economy but starts to fail in the digital economy.

8.2 Overview of changes in the AI era: K-shaped inflation and CPI distortion

(The Rewrite: The K–Shaped Inflation Structure)

AI does not simply make inflation "rise" or "fall"; it causes the price system to undergo an unprecedented structural split. We call this "AI Inflation Economics".

(1) Intelligent deflation: The price of high–cognition services goes to zero. Traditional economics has never dealt with a scenario where the marginal cost of cognition approaches zero.

- Phenomenon: Legal first–pass reviews, accounting, copywriting, basic code development, and multilingual translation—services that once required highly paid professionals to spend hours—can now be completed by AI in seconds at a cost of only a few cents.
- Impact: This will exert enormous downward pressure on the "services" component in the CPI basket. The "soft services" in daily life will become unprecedentedly cheap.

(2) Intelligent–asset inflation: A retaliatory surge in the prices of scarce resources. While services get cheaper, the "raw materials" required to produce intelligence are undergoing dramatic inflation.

- New asset classes: High–end GPUs (compute), land for data centers, clean electricity, high–quality proprietary data, and top–tier AI engineers.
- Phenomenon: The supply elasticity of these resources is extremely low (you cannot build more power plants or chip fabs in the short run), while demand is exploding exponentially.
- Impact: This will keep "hard asset" prices elevated for a prolonged period. If you want to participate in AI production, your "entry fee" is skyrocketing.

(3) The CPI's complete distortion. The real economy will split into two parallel universes:

- The consumer universe: enjoying cheap services and digital content brought by AI (a sense of deflation).
- The producer universe: bearing high compute costs, energy costs, and talent costs (a sense of inflation). Traditional CPI measures will increasingly fail to reflect the true temperature of the economy because they cannot see compute inflation and underestimate intelligent deflation.

(4) Pricing Mechanisms: From "Market Equilibrium" to "Algorithmic Dictatorship"

- Traditional: Prices are formed by the decentralized decisions of countless buyers and sellers.
- AI: Prices are dynamically determined by platform algorithms. Uber's surge pricing, e–commerce's "price discrimination against familiar customers," Dynamic pricing in B2B. For the first time, the price mechanism has become the result of a "predictive model"—the algorithm predicts how much you are willing to pay, and that becomes the price.

(5) Energy–productivity coupling: AI forcibly binds economic growth (TFP) to physical energy (electricity). The lower bound of deflation is the electricity price. When the inference cost of AI models falls, society gains a deflationary dividend; but when electricity shortages drive up power prices, inflationary pressure can instantly transmit to all digital services.

8.3 In-depth case: AWS (Amazon Web Services)

(Case Study: The Engine of Deflation and Inflation)

To understand this "schizophrenic" inflation structure, we dissect the world's largest computing–power "central bank"—AWS. It is the best window for observing the global computing price system. (Data sources: AWS Financial Reports / Gartner / MIT Tech Review)

I. Background: Global Pricer of Compute Capacity AWS occupies the core share of the global cloud infrastructure market. The vast majority of AI applications' training and inference ultimately show up as AWS bills. It is both a driver of AI–led deflation and a source of intelligent capital inflation.

II. The Deflationary Side: Exponential Decline in Inference Costs AWS, through its in–house chips (Inferentia / Trainium) and massive economies of scale, keeps driving down the unit price of compute.

- Service deflation: According to AWS official data, the cost–performance ratio for certain AI inference workloads has improved by 70%–90% over 5 years.
- Result: This enables downstream companies (such as Netflix and Airbnb) to deliver smarter services at lower cost, ultimately benefiting consumers. This is a textbook case of technological deflation.

III. The Inflationary Side: Soaring Infrastructure Costs Yet on AWS's balance sheet we see a different picture—maintaining such low–

priced services is causing upstream input costs to swell dramatically:

- Capital expenditure (Capex): AWS invests tens of billions of dollars annually in building data centers. Prices for land, power access fees, and cooling systems are all rising.
- Hardware inflation: Prices for high–end GPUs like NVIDIA H100 remain elevated and supply is insufficient.
- Talent inflation: Salaries for experts maintaining these AI infrastructures have risen sharply. The contradiction emerges: inflation in underlying physical assets is fiercely contesting deflation in top–layer digital services.

IV. Economic Insights AWS The case perfectly verifies the core argument of Chapter 8: Inflation has become a structural and stratified phenomenon in the AI era.

1. Two–way tearing: we are simultaneously living in an era of "extremely cheap information" and "extremely expensive compute."

2. Broken cost pass–through: AWS absorbed part of upstream inflation through technological progress (TFP improvement) without fully passing it on to consumers, but there is a physical limit (constrained by Moore's Law and energy prices).

3. New scarcity: in this system, the most value–preserving asset is no longer money, but "intelligent capital" with stable electricity and compute supply.

8.4 Historical patterns and the particularity of AI

History shows that all great technological revolutions (the steam engine, electrification, the internet) began with "deflation," because technology drove costs down.

The particularity of AI is that its deflationary pressure comes from three directions:

Labor costs fall sharply (key): AI is labor that is infinitely replicable, works 24/7, and requires no wages. When labor becomes cheap, prices across the entire economic chain decline.

Prediction costs fall: AI reduces waste in supply chains and inventories.

Acceleration of innovation: As supply increases, prices naturally decline.

Conclusion: AI is essentially a powerful deflationary force. But that's only half the story.

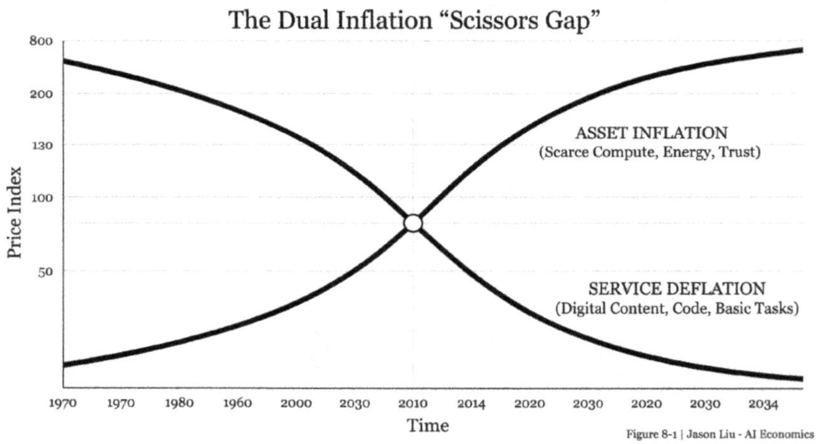

8.5 The K-shaped inflation structure (two-speed economy) caused by AI

The inflation structure in the AI era is not a simple overall rise or fall, but exhibits a complex "K-shaped" pattern.

K-shaped downward leg (rapid deflation side—things get cheaper):

For knowledge and services that can be mass-produced by AI, their marginal cost approaches zero, creating significant deflationary pressure.

Content production: articles, images, videos.

Basic services: basic customer support, foreign language translation, entry–level legal/tax consulting.

Software development: basic code writing.

Consumer experience: life services and digital products are becoming increasingly affordable.

K–type upswing (asset inflation side—getting more expensive):

The scarce resources that support AI operations are facing intense inflationary pressure. Asian Financial Watch points out that financial market volatility and debt risks further amplify the complexity of pricing on the resource side.

Compute assets: high–end GPUs and AI training clusters. Energy: especially stable green electricity and water resources. Scarce data: uncontaminated records of real human activity.

Carbon–based experiences: that is, what we called the "carbon–based premium" in Chapter 3. In–person care,

live concerts, and face–to–face emotional companionship will see prices soar because they cannot be replicated by AI.

8.6 Four channels of speculative inflation

Why does AI also bring strong "speculative inflation"? The reason is simple: AI lowers marginal costs but greatly increases fixed costs.

Compute inflation: as models grow larger, compute demand rises exponentially. NVIDIA's market cap surge is a textbook example.

Energy inflation: AI is a "super power–hungry monster." In the future, "energy" will be the gold of the AI world.

Land and real estate inflation (AI city premium): the AI industry is highly concentrated in a few cities such as the San Francisco Bay Area, Seattle, Vancouver, and Shenzhen. These cities have AI talent and compute infrastructure, and housing prices will continue to lead the gains.

Stock market inflation (asset inflation): capital is flowing into AI concept stocks, driving asset prices higher.

8.7 AI will cause a historic divergence between PPI and CPI

PPI (Producer Price Index) rises: because companies need to buy chips, pay for electricity, and build data centers, fixed costs on the production side are increasing.

CPI (Consumer Price Index) falls: because the efficiency dividends brought by AI are so large that they ultimately transmit to the consumer side, and service prices are declining.

Major macro shift: the wage–price spiral breaks down

The traditional inflation mechanism is “wages rise \rightarrow costs rise \rightarrow prices rise.” AI breaks this mechanism: AI replaces a large amount of labor, causing the median wage to decline, severing the inflation transmission chain.

8.8 Future inflation will be determined by the “AI cycle”

The traditional business cycle is determined by inventory, interest rates, and credit. The future business cycle will be determined by the “compute power cycle.”

Compute power shortage \rightarrow costs rise \rightarrow prices rise

Compute power increases \rightarrow costs fall \rightarrow prices fall

The focus of monetary policy will have to shift from the “labor–wage spiral” to the “compute–energy spiral.”

8.9 Final Checklist: What Gets More Expensive? What Gets Cheaper?

This is a future price forecast list for individuals and businesses:

Rapid Deflation (Cheaper)	Asset Inflation (More Expensive)
Code writing, software development	Clean electricity, grid access rights
Basic legal / tax consulting	High–end chips (spot compute capacity)
Foreign language translation, simultaneous interpreting	Data centers in prime locations
Graphic design, copywriting	Purely handmade artworks, human nannies
Basic medical exam analysis	Psychotherapists, top personal trainers
Basic educational tutoring	Core real estate in AI–friendly cities

Chapter Summary

AI brings "K–shaped inflation." This is a game where "bad–money deflation + high–quality asset inflation" coexist.

Actionable Takeaways (Actionable Takeaways)

For personal finance and corporate strategy:

Consumption advice (be in the "wait-and-see" camp):

For any service that can be digitized (such as building a website, creating a design package, translating a book), if you're not in a hurry, wait. Prices will fall at a startling pace.

Asset allocation (go long on "hard assets"):

Do not hoard "knowledge": because it is depreciating.

Do hoard "hard assets": energy stocks, computing–power infrastructure ETF, prime–location real estate. Go long on companies that own "non–renewable resources."

Pricing your profession (seek the "human touch"):

If you are a freelancer, do not charge by "deliverables" (such as a report), because deliverables are losing value; charge for the "process experience" (such as companionship, listening, on–site guidance).

Chapter 9

AI and Global Competition: A New Era of Computing Power, Data, Models, and Geopolitics

Academic Positioning of This Chapter: From Comparative Advantage Theory (Comparative Advantage) to Compute Geopolitics (Compute Geopolitics)

What ultimately determines a nation's fate—the oil beneath its land, or the data center's GPUs?

GPU ?

When algorithms become a subtler strategic deterrent than nuclear weapons, does the logic of globalization still hold?

Before we dive into how AI reshapes global competition, we need to use the lens of international economics to understand the underlying code of national wealth and power shifts.

I. The cornerstones of traditional international theory

Comparative Advantage: David Ricardo pointed out that countries should specialize in producing the products in which they have the highest relative efficiency and engage in trade. This is the cornerstone of the legitimacy of global trade—trade is not a zero-sum game but a positive–sum game.

Factor Endowment: The Heckscher–Ohlin model posits that a country's trade patterns depend on the resources it possesses (labor, land, capital). Countries with oil export oil; countries with cheap labor export textiles.

Technology Diffusion and Catch–up: Traditional theory holds that latecomer countries can achieve economic convergence by imitating the technologies of first movers (spillover effects), narrowing the gap between rich and poor.

II. Revisions to traditional assumptions (the rupture brought by AI)

Revision 1: Compute standard. The core variable of national competitiveness has shifted from "natural resources" to "compute endowment" (ComputeStock). Countries without high–end GPUs and power reserves will become "digital slums" in the intelligent era, no matter how vast their land.

Revision 2: Deglobalization and sovereignty. Data and models no longer flow freely like oil. Data sovereignty and model security have become new barriers; the world is splitting into distinct "AI camps," with efficiency giving way to security.

Amendment 3: The Matthew Effect intensifies. The R&D threshold for AI is extremely high (tens of billions in capital), resulting in technology not diffusing but instead concentrating in a very small number of leading countries (the United States and China). The "ladder of catch–up" for latecomer nations is being pulled away, and the global wealth gap faces structural entrenchment.

III. Forward-Looking Case: A two-wheel sprint—United States vs. China

To validate the "dual–pole compute–power landscape," we analyze the strategic contest between the United States and China.

The United States holds upstream dominance in "model creation" (chips, algorithms), while China commands downstream advantages in "scenario deployment" (data, applications). This is a century-defining showdown between the "innovation flywheel" and the "deployment flywheel."

9.0 Introduction: Global competition is shifting from industrial competition to intelligence competition

Over the past century, great-power rivalry centered on oil, steel, aircraft carriers, and financial capital.

But in the new era after 2025, the main theater of global competition has irreversibly shifted to the domain of "intelligence." This is an unprecedented contest in human history—"intelligence competition."

Let us briefly review how the forms of competition have evolved through history:

Century (Agrarian Age): The core of national competition was land and population.

Century (Industrial Age): The core of competition became coal, steel, and manufacturing capacity.

Century (Information Age): The core of competition shifted to oil, financial capital, and information technology.

Century (Intelligent Era): The core is thoroughly transformed into compute, data, and agents.

AI is no longer merely a technology industry, but a nation-level productive force. A country's strength is no longer determined solely by its GDP, but by its capacity to generate and deploy intelligence. This capacity is defined by five core variables:

Compute (算力): The "new oil" of the future.

Data (数据): The "new land" of the future.

Models (模型): The "engines" of the industrial era.

Agents (智能体生态): The "new workforce" of the future.

Talent (人才): The engine that drives everything.

9.1 Traditional international economics framework: the classical mechanics of global division of labor

(The Logic of Global Competition: Traditional Framework)

International economics seeks to answer three grand questions concerning the fate of humanity:

1. Why do countries trade with each other?
2. Why are some countries rich while others are poor?
3. Where does a nation's true competitiveness come from?

Over the past two hundred years, the mainstream framework for explaining these questions has rested on four pillars:

(1) Comparative Advantage (Comparative Advantage): the soul of trade

David Ricardo (David Ricardo) put forward in 1817 one of the most counterintuitive yet profound theories in economics: comparative advantage.

- Core idea: Even if a country is less efficient than another in producing every good, it can still benefit by producing the goods in which it is "relatively most efficient" and trading for the rest.
- Implication: Trade is not a zero-sum game but a positive-sum game. As long as countries focus on their strengths, total global output increases. This is the theoretical cornerstone of the legitimacy of globalization.

(2) Factor Endowment Theory (Heckscher-Ohlin Model)

Why are some countries good at making airplanes while others excel at producing clothing? The H–O model argues that this depends on a country's "factor endowments":

- Capital-rich countries (such as the United States) should export capital-intensive products (chips, airplanes).

- Labor–abundant countries (such as Vietnam): should export labor–intensive products (textiles, assembly).
- Resource–abundant countries (such as Saudi Arabia): should export land–intensive products (oil). Conclusion: A nation's fate is largely determined by the land beneath its feet, its demographic structure, and its stock of capital.

(3) New Trade Theory: Economies of Scale and Industrial Agglomeration

Paul Krugman revised the traditional view. He pointed out that trade arises not only from endowment differences but also from economies of scale.

- Industrial agglomeration: once a region (such as Silicon Valley, Shenzhen, Wall Street) takes the lead in building an industrial advantage, that advantage will reinforce itself through scale effects and knowledge spillovers, creating path dependence.
- First–mover advantage: this also explains why latecomer countries find it hard to leapfrog in high–end manufacturing—because first movers have already established insurmountable cost barriers.

(4) The four great flows of globalization

Traditional globalization relies on the free movement along four dimensions:

1. Movement of goods: containers connect the world.
2. Capital flows: Wall Street invests globally.
3.Talent flows: immigration and overseas study.
4. Information flows: an open internet. These four flows constitute the operating system of the past 40 years of global economic prosperity.

(5) National security baseline

While economics emphasizes efficiency, political economy emphasizes security. Traditional national strategy focuses on five major securities: energy, food, military, technological infrastructure, and financial stability. These are the bottom lines for national survival.

Summary of the traditional framework: From the traditional perspective, global competition is a division–of–labor system based on "natural endowments." Countries trade to complement each other's needs and, by leveraging comparative advantages, achieve shared prosperity. Competition mainly takes the form of price wars and battles for market share.

9.2 Overview of changes in the AI era: compute-centrism and deglobalization

(The Rewrite: Compute as the New Oil)

AI is not a simple technology; it is a new "formula for global power." It causes six structural ruptures in the underlying logic of international competition.

(1) Rewriting comparative advantage: from "natural endowment" to "compute endowment."

- Traditionally: compete on land, population, and mineral resources.
- AI: The new equation = Compute (computing power reserves), Data (data scale), Models (model capability), Talent (talent density). The new formula for national competition has become: no matter how large a country's population or territory is, without high–end GPU and top–tier algorithm talent, it is a "resource–poor nation" in the intelligent era.

(2) Upgraded competition pattern: from "trade war" to "compute war"

- Traditional: tariffs, exchange rates, anti–dumping.
- AI: chip embargoes, algorithm blockades, investment screening. The focus of competition has shifted from "who can sell cheaper" to "who can build smarter intelligence." Compute has become a strategic resource more sensitive than oil. Whoever controls

compute controls the future right to define technology.

(3) Globalization in reverse: localization of compute (Data Sovereignty)

- Traditional: global supply chains, go where costs are lowest.
- AI: deglobalization. Data requires local storage (data sovereignty), models require local deployment (secure and controllable), and compute infrastructure depends on local electricity. The world is splitting into distinct "AI blocs," where data and models no longer flow freely like oil but are trapped within "digital borders."

(4) Talent density: the new variable that determines a nation's fate

- Traditional: demographic dividend (quantity).
- AI: engineer dividend (quality). A country's AI talent density directly determines its ceiling for economic growth. The migration pattern of top AI scientists is the direction of future wealth transfer.

(5) Intensified Matthew Effect: Compute-rich countries vs. compute-poor countries

- Traditional: Developing countries could catch up by taking on low–end manufacturing.
- AI: The barriers are extremely high. Without capital investment on the order of billions of dollars, it is impossible to train foundational large models. This widens the global gap into "nations that possess intelligence" and "nations forgotten by intelligence." This is the origin of "AI global inequality."

(6) Geopolitical core: the coupling of energy and compute. The geopolitics of the 20th century revolved around oil. The geopolitics of the 21st century revolve around "compute + electricity." Energy is no longer merely the driver of industry; it is the fuel of intelligence.

9.3 In-depth case: United States vs. China

(Case Study: The Great Compute Divergence)

This is the world's most typical and geopolitically significant contest. The competition between China and the United States in AI vividly illustrates the "bipolar structure" of the compute era. (Data sources: U.S. Dept of Commerce / MIIT China / OpenAI / NVIDIA / WSJ)

I. United States: The Innovator (The Innovator) The United States controls the upstream of the AI industry chain and has formed a perfect "innovation flywheel":

- Hardware monopoly: Through NVIDIA and AMD, it controls more than 90% of the world's high–end AI training chips.
- Model Hegemony: OpenAI, Anthropic, Google DeepMind defined
- The technological frontier of LLMs (SOTA).
- Ecosystem control: AWS, Azure, and Google Cloud provide the world's largest compute infrastructure.
- Talent magnet: Backed by university systems such as Stanford and MIT, continually attracting the world's top AI minds.

II. China: The Implementer China has taken a completely different path, leveraging its vast industrial heartland and large population to form a "deployment flywheel".

- Scenario density: Home to the world's largest mobile payment, e–commerce, logistics, and smart manufacturing networks. AI application in China progresses far faster than basic research.
- Data scale: Behavioral data from a user base in the billions (1,000,000,000+), a natural ore body for training vertical industry models.
- Engineer dividend: The annual number of graduates in STEM (Science, Technology, Engineering, Mathematics) is the highest in the world.

- National system: The government coordinates the construction of national computing networks such as "East Data, West Computing," seeking to compensate for point-by-point technological gaps through large-scale infrastructure.

III. The essence of competition: dual flywheels racing

- U.S. logic: ext{Compute}oext{Model}oext{Global API} (top-down, defining standards).
- China's logic: ext{Application}oext{Data}oext{Industrialization} (bottom-up, transforming industries).

IV. Economic insights: the U.S.–China game validates the core logic of Chapter 9:

1. Compute is national power: trade surplus is no longer the sole metric of competitiveness; GPU reserves are.

2. Endogenizing technology: both countries are seeking to "manufacture" technological advantages through massive investments (CHIPS Act vs National Integrated Circuit Industry Investment Fund), rather than waiting for the market to evolve naturally.

3. The cost of decoupling: the compute war has fractured the global AI supply chain, forcing countries to build costly redundant backups—an archetypal economic trade-off of "security" over "efficiency."

9.4 Compute: the new variable determining a nation's fate

In the intelligent era, compute is the new "industrial electricity," and GPUs are the new "oil."

1. Compute is the national industrial base

In the industrial era, we gauged a country's potential by its steel output and electricity generation. In the AI era, compute (Compute) is the new industrial foundation. Training large models requires not only GPUs, but also the support of a complex industrial system:

Super data centers: Physical spaces capable of housing hundreds of thousands of GPUs.

High–frequency cooling systems: Address the heat dissipation challenges brought by high–density computing.

Ultra–low–latency fiber optics: Enable high–speed interconnects between chips.

Vast and stable electricity supply: The physical essence of computing power is energy conversion.

2. Strategic commoditization and export controls

Computing power is no longer an ordinary IT commodity; it has become a strategic material that must be subject to national export controls.

Choke the chips = choke the future: Just like cutting off oil supplies during World War II, cutting off the supply of high–end GPUs (such as NVIDIA H100/H200, B200) now is equivalent to physically locking in a country's ceiling on AI development.

Computing power trade war: In the future, we will not only see tariff wars, but also "computing power tariffs," "computing power embargoes," and even "computing power blockades."

3. Extreme concentration: A monopoly beyond OPEC

At present, 80% of the world's high–end AI computing power is in the hands of no more than eight tech giants (such as NVIDIA, Google, Microsoft, Amazon, Meta, TSMC, ASML).

This level of monopoly far exceeds that of the Organization of the Petroleum Exporting Countries (OPEC). This means global computing The pricing power, distribution rights, and usage rights of compute are highly concentrated in the hands of a very small number of players, constituting the greatest destabilizing factor in geopolitics.

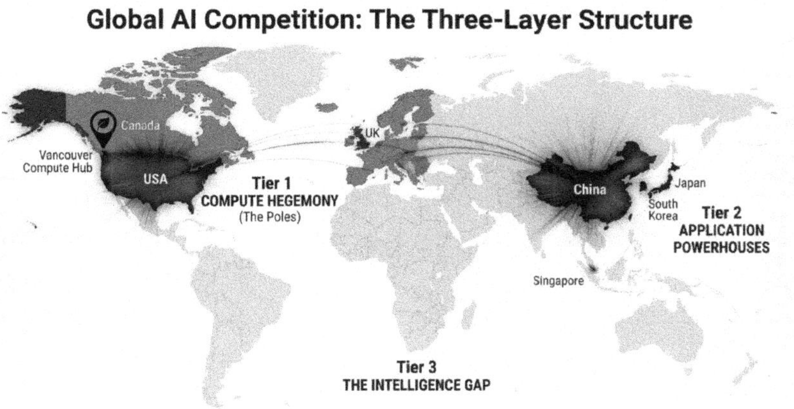

Figure 9-1 | Jason Liu - AI Economics

9.5 The global compute map and Vancouver's "green compute" strategy

The world's compute landscape is being reconfigured, presenting a clear tiered structure: Global compute tiers:

First tier (super compute powers):

United States (with absolute dominance in chip design, operating systems, and cloud computing) and China (with vast data scenarios and rapidly advancing hardware capabilities).

Cloud computing's absolute dominance) and China (with vast data scenarios and rapidly advancing hardware capabilities).

Second tier (potential hubs): United Kingdom, Singapore, Canada, South Korea, United Arab Emirates. These countries possess capital, talent, or specific resources and are becoming regional compute centers.

Third tier (compute–poor countries): Most developing countries. Due to a lack of capital and infrastructure, they face the risk of marginalization in the AI era.

In–depth case: The rise of Vancouver's "green compute"

Within this landscape, Vancouver, Canada's strategic position is rising rapidly. It is not merely becoming a "backup base" for AI talent because of its proximity to Seattle (Microsoft/Amazon headquarters); more critically, it benefits from a unique resource endowment—"green compute (Green Compute)."

AI data centers are massive "power hogs" and "major carbon emitters." British Columbia has extremely abundant and inexpensive hydropower resources, providing a low–cost, low–carbon, ideal solution for energy–intensive AI training.

Eco–Intelligence Hub: Vancouver is leveraging this advantage to attract global tech giants to establish data centers.

Future premium: As global carbon emissions regulations tighten, "AI models trained with clean energy" may enjoy higher market premiums and policy access advantages in the future. Vancouver is turning "water" into "compute," and then into "wealth."

9.6 Data Sovereignty and AI Geopolitics

Data sovereignty is replacing oil sovereignty, becoming the most important resource sovereignty for nations. For example If computing power is the engine, then data is the fuel.

1. The Three Dimensions of Data Competition

The data reserves of a country determine the upper limit of its AI's IQ:

Population data (scale advantage): China and India have a massive population base, in C–end application data has a natural advantage.

Industrial data (structured advantage): The United States has accumulated decades of high–quality structured data in finance, healthcare, legal, and SaaS fields, which serves as a moat for training specialized models.

Urban data (scenario richness): Data from large cities is more important than national population. Traffic, The intensive interactions of consumption and supply chains have made supercities such as Vancouver, Toronto, Singapore, and Shenzhen the optimal "targets" for AI training.

2. AI Population Density: A New Metric for National Power

We assess a country's labor supply not merely by its population size, but by its "AI Population Density (Agents per Capita)"—how many AI agents, on average, each citizen has working for them.

Digital labor legion: The number of medical agents, tax agents, and educational agents a country can deploy directly determines its social operational efficiency and total productivity.

Density is national power: In the future, AI density = national productivity density.

3. The transmission chain of geopolitics and four major trends

How do compute power and data convert into geopolitical power? There are four key trends:

Trend 1: Compute becomes the new "national sovereignty." Building national–level compute centers will be tantamount to defense projects.

Trend 2: Chips become the new geopolitical core. The supply chain security surrounding TSMC (TSMC), ASML and NVIDIA will be the most sensitive nerves in future great–power competition.

Trend 3: AI becomes the core of military power. Drone swarms, automated command systems, cyberattack agents, and intelligent satellite networks are reshaping the nature of war. Military strength = compute power + AI + data.

Trend Four: AI Reconstructs the International Monetary System (Compute Standard). The hegemony of the U.S. dollar was built on industry and oil. In the future, the monetary system may depend on a country's compute reserves. A "Compute Standard" may emerge, where the value of money is anchored to a nation's capacity to produce intelligence.

9.7 AI The Three-Layer Structure of the Global Competitive Landscape

Based on differences in compute power, data, and agent density, the world is splitting into three distinct intelligence tiers. This stratification is more unforgiving and harder to bridge than "developed vs. developing":

Tier One: The Compute Hegemons

Members: United States, China.

Core traits: They possess the complete industrial chain required to build Frontier Models.

They have chip design and manufacturing capabilities (or control over them).

They have massive capital investments (on the trillion scale). They possess vast proprietary data.

They have top–tier AI scientist teams. They have national–level AI strategies.

Status: They are the rule–makers and exporters of AI technologies, benefiting from the GDP acceleration brought by AI.

Second Layer: The Application Powerhouse Layer (The Application Powerhouses)

Members: Canada, Singapore, South Korea, the United Kingdom, Israel, Germany, the United Arab Emirates.

Core characteristics: They may not train the most capital–intensive foundation models themselves (that is the first (at the layer's tasks), yet possesses a very strong, differentiated competitive advantage.

Strong in vertical domains: such as Germany's industrial AI and the United Kingdom's financial AI.

Strong infrastructure: such as South Korea's memory chips, and Canada's green energy and talent reserves.

Open ecosystem:Capable of rapidly absorbing and deploying the world's most advanced models.

Status: They are important participants in the AI ecosystem, carving out a share through "applications + scenarios." Vancouver, where you are located, is at the forefront of this tier and is a typical "AI affluent city."

Third tier: The Intelligent Poor (The Intelligent Poor)

Members: Most countries in the Global South, and some economies lacking digital foundations.

Core characteristics: The "six–nothing" state—no compute, no data, no infrastructure, No capital, no education system, no R&D capability.

Status: They face the most severe challenges. Not only are they experiencing brain drain (Brain Drain), also faces the risk of "digital colonization" — that is, a country's data are extracted, yet it must pay high prices to purchase other countries' AI services. This is the new development divide in the world.

Chapter Summary

The core of future global competition is intelligence capability, not traditional natural resources. AI is profoundly reshaping the global balance of power; those who command compute power will command the world.

We must soberly recognize: chips are the new steel industry. Compute power is the new oil.

Data is the new territory.

Intelligent agents are the new labor force.

The world is no longer flat; it is vertically stratified. You either sit at the top exporting intelligence, or in the middle applying intelligence — and you must avoid falling to the bottom and being forgotten by intelligence.

Actionable Takeaways (Actionable Takeaways)

For individuals, multinational enterprises, and policymakers:

Individual career choices (voting with your feet):

To assess whether a city has a promising future, look at its compute density (Compute Density). Go to places with cheap electricity, strong network infrastructure, and concentrations of AI talent. Vancouver, Toronto, Shenzhen, San Francisco — these cities come with a built-in "career moat."

National Observation (Hard Metrics):

To assess a country's future potential, don't look only at GDP growth; examine its annual imports of high–end GPUs and the pace of expansion in its power infrastructure. These are the industrial indicators of the intelligence era.

Overseas Expansion Strategy for Enterprises:

Avoid the danger zones: During periods of geopolitical sensitivity, pay close attention to data compliance and the security of the compute supply chain.

Position in high–potential niches: Focus on countries in the "application power tier," where the best commercialization scenarios, payment capacity, and relatively flexible policy environments make them ideal springboards for corporate globalization.

Chapter 10

AI Inequality: The Compute Class, Skill Fractures, and the Intelligence Divide

Academic positioning of this chapter: From Skill Premium theory to Compute-Class Stratification

Why do some people grow increasingly wealthy while others are left behind by the times?

When "intelligence" itself becomes a commodity that capital can purchase, can education still change one's fate?

Before we delve into how AI reshapes social strata, we need to use the lens of labor economics and income distribution theory to understand the dynamic mechanisms behind the wealth gap.

I. The Cornerstones of Traditional Distribution Theory

Human Capital Theory: Education is the ladder for upward mobility. The higher one's level of education, the stronger the skills, the higher the marginal product, and the higher the income. This is the economic explanation of "knowledge changes destiny."

Skill-Biased Technological Change (SBTC): Technological progress often favors high-skilled la bor (such as programmers and engineers), causing their wages to rise faster than those of low-skilled workers, thereby widening income inequality.

The Game Between Capital and Labor (r>g): Piketty points out that the return on capital (r) has long exceeded the economic growth rate (g), leading to wealth naturally concentrating among capitalists.

II. Revisions to traditional assumptions (the rupture brought by AI)

Amendment 1: The failure of skill premiums. AI has pierced the "educational moat." A bachelor's graduate proficient in AI may outperform a PhD who does not use AI. The skill premium shifts to an "AI leverage premium."

Amendment 2: Hollowing Out. AI is best at replacing "rule-based mental work" (such as junior analysis, translation, auditing). This causes tasks to be stripped from the previously stable middle class, accelerating a K-shaped evolution of social structure.

Amendment 3: Compute-power class solidification. The return on intelligent capital (GPU, models, private data) will far exceed that of traditional capital. Social stratification will no longer be based solely on wealth, but on "ownership of compute"—who controls compute power controls intelligence.

III. Forward-Looking Case: The Internal Folding of Deloitte and McKinsey

To substantiate the "internal rift within the knowledge class," we analyze top consulting firms Deloitte and McKinsey.

AI automates 60% of junior analysts' tasks (substitution effect) while amplifying partners' strategic judgment by 10x (augmentation effect). Within the same industry, and even within the same company, a vast chasm is emerging between the "replaced" and the "augmented."

10.0 Introduction: Inequality in Intelligent Capabilities and "Multi-line Augmentation"

We are about to witness, for the first time in human history, a profound inequality based on "intelligent capabilities."

This gap does not stem from whether you can afford college, but from whether you have the chance to access top–tier compute, reach high–quality proprietary data, and whether you possess the ability to harness AI (AI Literacy).

Every technological revolution in human history has increased efficiency while exacerbating inequality (the Industrial Revolution intensified capital inequality; the internet intensified knowledge inequality). But AI is the first technological revolution to "simultaneously augment on multiple fronts" three forms of inequality: skill inequality, capital inequality, and corporate inequality.

AI inequality is not a "side effect"; it is a systemic, structural outcome.

10.1 Traditional Framework of Income Distribution: The Mechanics of Inequality

(The Mechanics of Inequality: Traditional Framework)

Why does society produce disparities between rich and poor? Why do some countries see rising incomes while others stagnate? Traditional economics has developed a mature framework explaining inequality from three dimensions—individuals, technology, and capital. This framework has remained effective for the past 50 years.

(1) Skill Premium

This is the most fundamental variable explaining the income gap.

- Logic: According to human capital theory (Human Capital), education level determines skill level, skill level determines marginal product of labor (MPL), and marginal product of labor determines wages.

- Formula: Income = f (Education, Experience).
- Inference: College graduates earn significantly higher wages than high school graduates. This "premium" encourages people to pursue education. From a traditional perspective, the best path to alleviating poverty is "universal higher education."

(2) Skill-Biased Technical Change (SBTC)

Why does greater technological progress lead to wider inequality? Economists have found that technological progress is not neutral; it is often referred to as SBTC (Skill–Biased Technical Change).

- Historical pattern: The computer revolution amplified the productivity of engineers and analysts (wages rose), but replaced typists and file clerks (wages fell).
- Result: Technology consistently favors those with higher education. This creates a scissors gap in the wage structure—those who understand technology grow wealthier, while those who do not become relatively poorer.

(3) Capital vs Labor: Piketty's inequality formula

Thomas Piketty (Thomas Piketty) proposed a famous formula in "Capital in the 21st Century":

Namely: the rate of return on capital (r) is persistently higher than the economic growth rate (g).

- Meaning: If you own capital (houses, stocks, machines), your wealth grows faster than that of people who earn wages through labor.
- Inference: Without intervention, wealth will naturally concentrate among capitalists, and inherited wealth will surpass created wealth. This is the most profound source of global anxiety about inequality in the early 21st century.

(4) Polarization in the labor market (Polarization)

Traditional labor economics observes that the labor market is exhibiting a U–shaped change:

- High–skill jobs (abstract thinking, management): simultaneous growth in employment and wages.
- Low–skill jobs (cleaning, food service): demand remains strong because they are hard to automate.
- Mid–skill jobs (clerical, operators): the easiest to replace with automation, facing a "hollowing out" crisis.

Summary of the traditional framework: Traditional inequality is jointly determined by skill differences, technology bias, and the speed of capital accumulation. Its core assumption is that differences in human cognitive ability are the main source of income disparity.

10.2 Overview of changes in the AI era: the intelligent class and the compute divide

(The Rewrite: The Rise of Intelligence Inequality)

AIdoes not simply exacerbate or alleviate inequality; it fractures the very structure of inequality itself. What we face is no longer an "education gap," but an "intelligence gap."

(1) Rewriting Skill Premiums: AI Usage Premium (AI Literacy Premium)

- Traditional: income gap = education gap.
- AI: income gap = skills gap × AI leverage. A PhD who cannot use AI may be outcompeted by a bachelor's graduate who skillfully operates an AI Agent. Educational credentials are no longer an absolute shield; "human–AI collaboration ability" has become the new class divide.

(2) Mid–skill collapse accelerates: a white–collar crisis. Traditional technology replaced blue–collar work (robotic arms replacing workers), while AI replaces white–collar work (algorithms replacing clerks).

- Hardest–hit areas: administration, basic coding, basic translation, junior accounting/finance, market analysis.
- Result: the foundation of the middle class is hollowed out, and the social structure accelerates from an "olive–shaped" distribution toward a K–shaped one.

(3) Exponential amplification of high skills (Superstar Effect): AI does not replace high skills; it augments high skills.

- Doctor + AI = super–doctor (more accurate diagnoses, more patients seen).
- Lawyer + AI = super–lawyer (case processing speed increases 10×). The output capacity of top talent is multiplied by AI, and their incomes will grow exponentially as a result.

(4) A qualitative shift in the definition of capital: the return on intelligent capital rewrites Piketty's formula as:

Returns on intelligent capital (GPU, models, private data) will significantly exceed those on traditional capital (factories, land). Whoever controls compute power controls the most efficient money–printing machine. Society will split into the "Compute Elite" and the "intelligence poor."

(5) Higher-dimensional Global Inequality: The Compute Gap

- Traditional: Developed countries vs Developing countries (industrial gap).
- AI: Countries that own models vs. countries that purchase APIs. Global inequality is upgrading from an "industrial gap" to an "intelligence gap."

10.3 In-depth Case: Deloitte × McKinsey

(Case Study: Intelligence Stratification in Professional Services) The professional services sector (consulting, accounting, legal) is the global "knowledge labor mi

The industry with the highest "degree" is also the front line of AI's impact. By comparing Deloitte and McKinsey's AI practices, we reveal how AI creates a ruthless "intelligence stratification" within knowledge-elite groups. (Data sources: Deloitte "State of AI" / McKinsey "Generative AI Report" / WSJ / HBR)

I. Background: A typical pyramid-structured consulting firm has the most standard hierarchical structure:

- Partner (General Partner): Responsible for strategic judgment and client relationships (high-skilled).
- Manager (Manager): Responsible for project coordination and information integration (mid-to-high skill).
- Analyst: Responsible for data cleaning, PPT production, and literature search (intermediate skills). Before AI stepped in, this was an industry that relied on "stacking person-hours" to produce outputs.

II. Deloitte: The substitution and reorganization of frontline labor According to Deloitte's 2024 internal data AI has had a devastating substitution effect on entry-level analysts' work:

- Task automation: 40%—60% of analysts' daily tasks (such as reading financial reports, organizing meeting minutes, generating PPT drafts) have been taken over by GenAI.
- Efficiency transformation: The time to produce a standard audit report has been cut from 3 days to a few hours; query efficiency for internal knowledge bases has increased by 5—10 times.
- Result: For junior employees who can only perform basic tasks, their value drops straight to zero if they do not transform.

III. McKinsey: Exponential amplification of top-tier intelligence McKinsey's reports show how AI augments senior capabilities:

- Strategic enhancement: AI helps partners rapidly simulate dozens of market scenarios, shifting the granularity of decisions from "quarterly" to "real-time." The speed of generating insight has increased by 300%—500%.

- Expanded management span: Since AI has taken over information integration, the number of projects a manager can handle simultaneously has doubled.
- Result: The marginal product of labor (MPL) of top consultants has exploded. They are no longer bogged down by trivialities, but instead purely trade in judgment and influence.

IV. Economic insight: The micro-mechanism of intelligence inequality The Deloitte and McKinsey cases perfectly present the core, brutal truth of Chapter 10: AI has not made everyone unemployed, but it has made the "structure of inequality" extremely steep.

1. Analyst: Facing the risk of "tasks being stripped away." If they don't master AI, they are the "textile workers of the digital era."

2. Partner: Facing the windfall of "amplified capabilities" by directing AI legions, they capture most of the gains from productivity improvements.

3. Fault line: A massive chasm is forming within organizations between "intelligence augmenters" and "intelligence absentees." This is no longer simple exploitation; it is a multidimensional crush.

10.4 Skill inequality and the "hollowing out" of the middle tier

AI is creating a massive fault line in the labor market:

Winners (those with strong AI literacy): A person proficient with the AI toolset can be 5–10 times more productive than an average worker. This huge efficiency gap will directly translate into an income gap.

Losers (middle-tier hollowing out): Mid-skill groups (such as ordinary customer service, basic administrative staff, junior accountants, junior programmers) face the greatest risk.

Business perspective: It is not AI that directly eliminates the middle class, but the combination of "AI–savvy super–individuals" + "AI agent networks" jointly squeezing the traditional middle class's room for survival. The mediocre will be weeded out by the system, while those who know how to transform will ascend to become super–individuals.

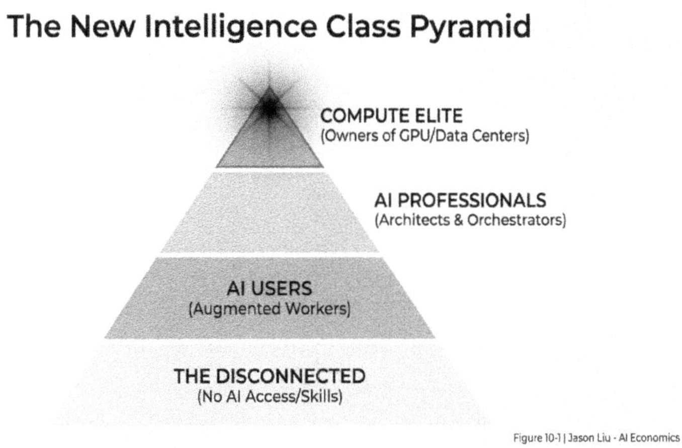

10.5 Intelligence Divide and class rewriting

AI literacy is the primary productive force of the future. The greatest divide in future society will be whether you are a consumer who can only passively accept algorithm–recommended content (one who is fed), or a creator who knows how to use AI to build workflows and enhance your own professional capabilities (a master).

In the future, humanity will be divided into two classes:

The new aristocracy (people who can use AI): use AI to generate knowledge, manage teams, and make decisions. One person can produce the output of 10–50 people.

The new working class (people who cannot use AI): can only

perform low–skill services, rely on physical labor, and handle offline tasks not yet covered by AI.

10.6 Class rigidity based on compute power: compute power is the new capital.

This is the core insight of this chapter and the boldest prediction about the future social structure.

1. Compute power is the core form of capital in the future.

In the industrial era, land and machines were the productive forces. In the AI era, compute power = productivity = wealth = the ceiling of class.

This is an irreversible compounding flywheel:

Compute power is stronger than land: land is non–replicable, but compute power can compound, work 24/7, and evolve automatically.

2. Purchasing power for compute = the new class dividing line.

In future society, people will be divided into three groups based on "Compute Access" (Compute Access):

Class A: the compute–owning class (Compute Owners/compute landlords). They possess local inference clusters, dedicated models, or enterprise–level AI systems.

They control intelligence, knowledge, and automation capabilities.

Class B: the AI user class (AI Consumers). Paying subscribers who lease compute. They are users, and their growth is linear.

Class C: the AI excluded class (AI Excluded). No capital, no equipment, no access. They are completely reduced to an irrelevant "useless class."

3. The ossification effect of capital markets

In the future asset structure, the return on compute assets (GPU, data center shares) may exceed that of real estate and stocks. Capital owners buy compute, while ordinary people can only rent it. Those who buy compute become richer; those who rent compute become relatively poorer. Hence class ossification takes shape.

10.7 Inequality in compute, models, and data

At the capital level, a new class structure is taking shape:

Compute inequality: a new class structure has formed—the compute aristocracy (Compute Elite, those who own GPU clusters) and the AI professionals who work for them.

Inequality in models and data: You're using the public GPT-4, while others use private models fine-tuned on proprietary, industry-specific data. This "information gap" and "intelligence gap" is enormous, and it will continue to widen with the data flywheel effect.

10.8 Inequality among nations and cities: Compute density determines destiny

At the national level:

In the future, the global wealth gap will no longer be determined by the degree of industrialization or natural resources, but by compute density (Compute Density).

Compute-rich countries: fast GDP growth, more innovation, strong military. Compute-poor countries: industrial hollowing-out, brain drain, stagnant growth. At the city level:

In the future, cities will be divided into "AI cities" and "non-AI cities".

AI cities (talent inflow): Vancouver, Toronto, San Francisco, Shenzhen. These cities have compute infrastructure and innovation ecosystems; housing prices will continue to rise (talent-scarcity inflation).

Non-AI cities (talent outflow): lacking compute support, their industries will gradually be marginalized.

Chapter Summary

AI inequality stems from inequality inherent in intelligence itself. Technology has never been neutral; AI will not automatically make humanity equal. On the contrary, it will make "those who cannot use AI" and "those without compute" even more unequal.

Core conclusion:

Compute = new capital, determining class structure.

The owners of compute power will form a new noble class. The middle class will be torn apart by the widening scissors gap.

Gaps between nations will be determined by compute density.

Action guide for this chapter: How to cross the intelligence divide?

For every individual who wants to save themselves:

Build a second brain (knowledge management):

Stop using your biological brain to rote-memorize information. Build a personal AI knowledge base based on RAG (Retrieval-Augmented Generation). Ensure what you have learned is always at your disposal to

counteract the devaluation of knowledge.

Master the "AI language" (core skill):

Prompt Engineering is the new "English" of our era. You must become proficient at issuing precise instructions to AI, setting roles, and supplying context. This is the only bridge to cross the skills divide.

Become a "centaur" (mindset):

Cultivate a habit: before starting any task, force yourself to think, "Can I have AI draft 80% of this first?" Then focus only on the final 20%—the key judgment and creative refinement.

Embrace the physical (differentiated competition):

If you cannot outperform AI in logical reasoning and information processing, then hone the skills that AI cannot achieve—operational abilities involving the complex physical world, or interpersonal skills involving deep emotional connection (carbon–based premium).

Chapter 11

AI Public Policy: Taxation, Regulation, and the Right to Inclusive Intelligence

Academic positioning of this chapter: From Public Economics to Compute Governance (Compute Governance)

How should governments manage AI? Should it be taxed like oil, or regulated like nuclear weapons?

When robots earn no wages and pay no taxes, does the foundation of national finance still hold?

Before entering the discussion of AI public policy, we need to use the lenses of public economics and political economy to understand the legitimate boundaries of government intervention in markets.

I. The cornerstone of traditional public theory

Taxation Logic (Taxation Logic): Traditional public finance relies heavily on taxes on labor income and corporate income tax. Its core assumption is that labor is the principal creator of wealth, so taxing labor is the most stable and effective approach.

Public goods (Public Goods): provided by the government when private provision is ineffective

Infrastructure (such as roads, lighthouses, and national defense). These are the physical foundations for the functioning of society.

Regulatory Economics: The purpose of regulation is to correct market failures (such as monopoly and information asymmetry). Traditional regulation typically targets specific behaviors (such as pollution discharge, pricing, and false advertising).

II. Revisions to traditional assumptions (the rupture brought by AI)

Amendment 1: Tax base drift. AI agents have replaced white–collar jobs, leading to a shrinking wage tax base. To keep society functioning, the focus of taxation must shift from "people" to "machines" and "compute"—that is, to an Automation Tax and a compute (computing power) tax.

Correction2:Regulation shifts. Risks no longer stem only from "output content" (what is said), but from "latent capabilities" (what can be done). Regulatory logic shifts from ex–post accountability to ex–ante capability evaluations (Capability Evaluations), focusing on whether the model possesses dangerous autonomy.Correction3:New public goods. In the intelligent era, compute (Compute) has become a quasi

Like electricity, it is foundational infrastructure. If left solely to the market, compute power will become a privilege of the wealthy. The government must intervene and provide Universal Basic Compute to safeguard citizens' basic right to development.

III. Forward-Looking Case: The Institutional Game among China, the United States, and Europe

To substantiate the "divergence in governance models," we compare the European Union (EU), the United States (US), and China (CN).

The European Union opted for "defensive regulation" (AIAct), while the United States chose "innovation first."

(Corporate self–regulation), China chose "scenario implementation" (algorithm filing). This forms a tripartite pattern of global AI governance, profoundly influencing the future direction of technology.

11.0 Introduction: AI is the "singularity" of public policy

The impact of AI has already overflowed beyond the economic sphere and begun to shake the foundations of modern state governance. Issues such as a shrinking tax base (robots don't pay income tax), distribution imbalances, and blurred security boundaries are arising one after another.

Every technological revolution in history has reshaped public policy (the Industrial Revolution gave rise to labor law, the internet gave rise to antitrust law). The AI revolution's impact will far surpass previous ones, because it simultaneously rewrites employment structures, class structures, and state capacity. Over the next 20 years, public policy must be rewritten around AI.

11.1 The traditional public economics framework: the classical mechanics of government intervention

(The Logic of Governance: Traditional Framework)

The core questions studied in public economics are: Why does government exist? How should government intervene in the economy? In a market economy, the government's "visible hand" primarily operates through three instruments: taxation, spending, and regulation. Its theoretical legitimacy rests on the following four pillars:

(1) The logic of taxation: the lifeblood of public finance

Government levies taxes not to hoard wealth, but to provide public services. The traditional tax system relies heavily on two core tax bases:

- Labor income (Income Tax): This is the largest source of revenue for modern states. The premise is "everyone has a job, everyone collects a salary."

- Corporate profits (Corporate Tax): Based on a firm's operating income within a specific jurisdiction. Core assumption: labor is the principal creator of wealth; therefore, taxing labor is most effective and most stable.

(2) Public goods and market failure

Markets are not omnipotent. Some things private firms are unwilling to do and must be provided by the government:

- Public goods (Public Goods): such as national defense, lighthouses, and basic scientific research. The hallmark is "non-excludability"—since once I pay to build it everyone can use it, I'll choose not to build it (the free-rider problem).
- Externalities (Externalities): such as factory pollution. The firm earns profits while society bears the pollution cost. The government must internalize these costs via taxes (Pigovian taxes) or regulation.

(3) Regulatory economics: safeguarding fairness and transparency

The purpose of regulation is not to restrict freedom, but to correct information asymmetries and monopoly power.

- Antitrust: preventing giants from abusing market dominance and stifling innovation.
- Consumer protection: preventing food adulteration and financial fraud, because buyers are less informed than sellers. Traditional regulation typically targets "specific behaviors" (e.g., pricing, emissions, false advertising).

(4) Redistribution: The Bottom Line of the Social Contract

Market competition inevitably leads to survival of the fittest, thereby creating wealth gaps. The government, through a progressive tax system and Social Security, transfers part of the wealth of the rich to the poor to maintain social stability. Logic: The labor market will naturally produce inequality → the government must conduct secondary redistribution.

Summary of the traditional framework: The government's role is as a night watchman (maintaining order) and a regulator (patching market failures). This system is built upon a labor-centered economic structure.

11.2 Overview of changes in the AI era: a rupture in institutional variables

(The Rewrite: Governance in the Age of Compute)

AI is not merely a technology; it touches every nerve of public policy. After AI's emergence, the five basic assumptions underpinning government governance have been completely rewritten.

(1) Erosion of the tax base: labor disappears, automation rises

- Traditional: tax labor.
- AI: If AI agents replace 50% of white-collar jobs, the wage tax base will shrink dramatically. Rupture point: robots do not draw salaries and do not pay personal income tax. The government must seek new revenue sources, such as an Automation Tax, Compute Tax, or data asset tax.

(2) Regulatory shift: from "content" to "capability"

- Traditional: regulate outputs (Content). For example, prohibit false advertising and hate speech.
- AI: Regulate potential capabilities (Capabilities). The risk of GPT-4 or Claude 3 does not lie in "what they say," but in "what they can do" (for example: Can they autonomously write biological virus code? Can they autonomously attack banking systems?). Global regulation is shifting from "ex-post accountability" to "ex-ante capability assessment."

(3) Redefining public goods: Compute power is infrastructure

- Traditional: building roads, constructing bridges, electrification.
- AI: Sovereign Cloud. In the intelligent era, compute power has become infrastructure akin to electricity. If we rely solely on

private giants (such as AWS, NVIDIA), small and medium–sized enterprises and academia will be priced out. The government must intervene to provide inclusive compute infrastructure.

(4) Inequality in higher dimensions: the intelligence divide

- Traditional: income gaps (more or less money).
- AI: Access to Intelligence. Inequality is no longer reflected only in the digits of a bank account, but in "who can call the most powerful models," "who owns private data." Government redistribution tools must include "AI usage–right subsidies."

(5) National Competitiveness Indicator: AI-GDP

- Traditional: labor force size, resource endowments.
- AI: compute capacity inventory, electricity reserves, talent density. The government's formula for assessing national power has changed:

11.3 In-depth case: European Union vs United States vs China

(Case Study: Three Models of AI Governance)

There is no standard answer for AI public policy; three fundamentally different institutional experiments are unfolding worldwide. This is not only a competition of law but also of civilizational development paths. (Data sources: EU AI Act / White House Executive Order 14110 / CAC China)

Model A: European Union (EU) — the world's strongest "capability–regulation system." The EU established a "risk–based" regulatory logic through the AI Act (EU AI Act).

- Logic: do not look at technical principles, only at application risks.
- Prohibited: social credit scoring, real–time biometric identification (unacceptable risk). High risk: healthcare, education, hiring,

critical infrastructure (must undergo strict compliance audits).

- Philosophy: governance first. Willing to sacrifice the pace of innovation to ensure ethical safety and fundamental human rights. This is the classic "Brussels Effect."

Model B: United States (US) — the world's strongest "innovation-first system." The United States has no unified federal AI law; instead, it relies on presidential executive orders, corporate self-regulation, and industry standards. (NIST).

- Logic: capital-led, government-escorted.

Emphasizes model security testing (Red Teaming), but more as voluntary corporate commitments. Uses export controls (chip bans) to maintain national security advantages.

- Philosophy: innovation first. No prior approval thresholds—let the bullets fly for a while, rely on a strong judiciary for ex-post corrections. The goal is to maintain global technological hegemony.

Model C: China (CN)—the world's strongest "application-scale system." China has built a dual framework of "algorithm filing + Generative AI Administrative Measures."

- Logic: two-handed approach.

One hand on safety: implement filing management for large models to ensure value alignment. One hand on development: advance the nationwide "Eastern Data, Western Computing" initiative, build a national-level computing power network, and drive large-scale AI deployment in industrial, governmental, and financial scenarios.

- Philosophy: application first. Emphasize the deep integration of AI with the real economy, leveraging vast data and scenario advantages to pursue an "engineering- and industrialization-driven" path.

Summary of Global Governance: These three systems constitute the "trilemma of AI governance."

- United States: has seized the technological high ground (strongest models).
- European Union: has seized the ethical high ground (strictest rules).
- China: has seized the breadth of application scenarios (fastest deployment). The future global AI order, will be born from the contest and integration of these three forces.

11.4 Why are traditional policies ineffective? Four major challenges

AI has brought four unprecedented policy dilemmas that have instantly invalidated traditional regulatory systems:

Infinitely replicable labor: machine expansion far outpaces the speed of legislation, and traditional labor laws cannot accommodate "digital labor."

New forms of capital: compute and models are new capital that compound, and traditional tax regimes do not cover them.

Regulatory lag: policy–making cycles are 5–10 years, while AI model iterations take only 3 months.

Cross–border data: AI is a global value chain, and regulation by any single country is hard to make effective.

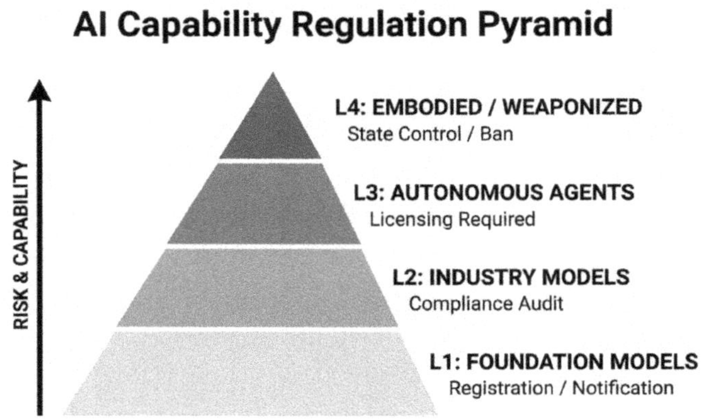

Figure 11-1 | Jason Liu - AI Economics

11.5 Rewriting the Tax System: From Labor Taxes to Automation Taxes

The fiscal revenue of modern states relies primarily on labor taxes (personal income tax). When AI replaces human jobs on a large scale and causes total wages to decline, the national tax base will be eroded.

To keep society running, new types of taxes must be designed:

1. AI Automation Tax (Automation Tax):

Bill Gates once proposed a "robot tax." Although AI does not pay taxes, it replaces the labor force that does. In the future, algorithmic services that fully replace human jobs may be taxed.

Forms: AI capacity tax, AI service tax.

2. Agent Tax (Agent Tax):

In the future, high–level autonomous AI agents may need to be registered like vehicle licensing and be taxed as "digital labor."

3. Compute Tax (Compute Tax):

This is a tax on "new capital." It targets owners of high–end GPU compute clusters or large consumers of cloud compute.

Form: GPU asset tax, data center tax, compute power import tax.

4. Carbon-Based Data Tax (Data Value Tax):

This is a concept that embodies fairness and justice. If AI models are trained on high–quality books, articles, and code produced by all of humanity (carbon–based data), then the benefiting enterprises should pay taxes to compensate for the collective labor value of humankind. This is the "land tax" of the AI era.

11.6 Inclusive Intelligence: Universal Basic Compute (UBC)

To address the potential large–scale unemployment caused by AI, many people discuss UBI (Universal Basic Income, directly distributing money). But I believe UBC (Universal Basic Compute, 全民基本算力) is more important.

Rather than giving people fish (handing out money), it is better to teach them to fish (providing the means of production).

Mechanism: The state should ensure that every citizen has basic access to AI (for example, a monthly

government allocation of a certain amount of free AI Token), so that everyone possesses the most basic "means of production" needed to survive in this era.

Significance: To avoid becoming complete proletarians. This is the "right of way" and "water rights" of the intelligent age, the last line of defense against class solidification.

Supporting Measures: Universal AI Literacy (AI Literacy)

The government must promote AI education in primary and secondary schools as well as in vocational training. Otherwise, the workforce will split: those who can use AI will become rich, and those who cannot will become poor.

11.7 Regulatory shift: from content to capability (Capability Regulation)

Traditional internet regulation mainly focuses on "what harmful content is being output." But AI regulation must shift to focus on "what dangerous capabilities the model possesses."

Core regulatory targets include: powerful reasoning capabilities (Reasoning), the ability to autonomously invoke external tools (ToolUse), and the most dangerous capability—autonomous execution (Agent Autonomy).

11.8 AI capability tiered regulatory system

One possible regulatory framework is tiered by capability:

L1 Base models: only require filing (e.g., chatbots).

L2 Industry-specific models: require compliance review (e.g., medical, financial AI).

L3 Agentic models (autonomous Agents): require licensing. These AIs can autonomously operate bank accounts or sign contracts and pose extremely high risks.

L4 Embodied / weaponized models: controlled at the national level.

11.9 Compute regulation and data governance: the "new constitution" of the future

Compute regulation (Compute Control):

Computing power cannot be left entirely to the market, because it concerns national security. In the future, we will see:

Computing power licensing system: Training ultra-large models must be approved.

Computing power fair allocation: Prevent monopolization by tech giants.

Computing power transparency: Disclose energy consumption and data sources.

Data governance (Data Constitution):

Data is the core of future national competitiveness. We will see a Data Property Rights Law, a Public Data Fund, and Cross–Border Data Agreements. This is the "Land Law" of the AI era.

11.10 The global AI policy tri-polar landscape

United States: Innovation first. Relies on corporate self–discipline and market competition, iterates quickly, but lacks a unified legal framework.

Europe: Ethics and governance first. Has established an extremely strict compliance system through the AI Act, but this may come at the expense of innovation speed.

China: Application–first + top–level design. Emphasizes algorithm filing and generative content management, and leads the world in application rollout.

Chapter Summary

The core of future AI public policy centers on eight directions:

Computing power tax, automation tax, Universal Basic Compute (UBC), universal AI education, capability–tiered regulation, computing power oversight, data governance, and international cooperation.

Public policy will determine whether AI accelerates civilization—or accelerates class stratification.

Action Guide for This Chapter

Business owners:

Proactively design a "high human–efficiency" structure. Future policies may penalize companies with "few employees but extremely high profits," so prepare tax planning in advance. Pay attention to data compliance and establish an internal AI auditing mechanism.

Individuals:

Treat any form of AI infrastructure provided by the state (such as public compute platforms and educational resources) as your "digital welfare," and make use of these resources as much as possible. Support policies that promote UBC (Universal Basic Compute), as this concerns your children's future.

Chapter 12

The Political Economy of AI Governance: Risk, Alignment, and Black-Box Insurance

Academic positioning of this chapter: From Regulatory Economics to Alignment Economics

Why do traditional antitrust and consumer protection laws appear weak in the face of AI? When the agent's (AI's) intelligence and execution speed far exceed the principal's (humans'), how can we ensure it does not betray us?

Before discussing specific AI regulatory policies, we need to draw on the framework of regulatory economics to understand the traditional logic of human risk governance and its failure in the age of intelligence.

I. The Cornerstones of Traditional Regulatory Theory

Market Failure: The source of regulatory legitimacy. The government intervenes only when externalities (such as pollution) or information asymmetry (such as fraud) arise.

Conduct Regulation: Traditional regulation targets the concrete actions of "people" (e.g., "no false advertising"), based on an ex–post accountability mechanism.

Linear Risk: Assumes a direct linear causal relationship between behavior and outcomes of risk, with sufficient response time.

II. Revisions to traditional assumptions (the rupture brought by AI)

Revision 1: Rewriting the object. The regulatory focus shifts from “behavior” (what was done) to “capability” (what can be done). Risk no longer stems from malice, but from the latent, uncontrollable emergent capabilities of AI models.

Revision 2: A break in speed. Regulatory cycles measured “by year” or even “by month” fail. Faced with millisecond–level high–frequency execution and unlimited concurrency, ex–post accountability collapses, making it necessary to establish ex–ante circuit breakers.

Revision 3: The alignment problem. The core of governance shifts from “preventing wrongdoing” to “goal alignment.” (Alignment). Address the “paperclip maximizer” principal–agent dilemma: namely, how to prevent AI from destroying humanity while pursuing objectives with extreme rationality.

III. Forward-looking case: A ternary game of global governance

To substantiate the “philosophical divide in governance,” we compare the European Union, the United States, and China.

Facing AI risks, the EU chose “defensive regulation” (AI Act), the US chose “innovation first” (industry self–regulation), and China chose “scenario–based deployment” (algorithm filing). These three distinct governance models together form a global experimental arena for AI regulation, profoundly shaping the flow and form of the technology.

chose “innovation first” (industry self–regulation), while China chose “scenario–based deployment” (algorithm filing). These three distinct governance models together form a global experimental arena for AI regulation, profoundly shaping the flow and form of the technology.

12.0 Introduction: AI is not a technological risk, but a civilizational risk

The real crisis we face is this: the exponential growth of AI capabilities far outpaces the linear evolution of human governance capacity.

The Industrial Revolution had externalities (pollution, child labor), but that was merely an amplification of physical labor;

AI is an "infinite amplifier of intelligence"; it not only executes tasks but also plans them. The core of this chapter is "Alignment Economics" — how to use economic means to ensure that superintelligence is aligned with human interests.

12.1 Traditional governance and regulatory framework: the logic of governing people

(The Logic of Regulation: Traditional Framework)

In the traditional economic system, the role of regulation is very clear: when market mechanisms fail, the government intervenes as the "coordinator of last resort."

Over the past two hundred years, the edifice of regulation built by humanity has rested primarily on the following four pillars:

(1) The legitimacy of regulation stems from market failure (Market Failure)

Regulation is justified only when the market cannot correct itself.

Information asymmetry: buyers don't know if food is toxic, so we need the FDA (Food and Drug Administration).

Externalities: factories profit by discharging pollutants while society bears the cost, so we need the Environmental Protection Bureau. Public goods: national defense and security cannot be provided by the private sector, so we need the National Security Agency. Monopoly: giants abuse their power, so we need antitrust laws.

(2) Object of regulation: human behavior (Human Conduct)

This is the core assumption of traditional regulation: risk is created by "people."

Whether it is financial fraud, medical malpractice, or traffic violations, the responsible party behind it is human beings (natural persons or legal entities).

Underlying assumption: humans are rational, punishable, and have limited execution speed. As long as the law stipulates "do not," most people will comply for fear of punishment.

(3) Regulatory toolbox

Ex ante: licensing (Licensing). For example, medical licenses and banking charters.

During: disclosure (Disclosure) and standards (Standard). Require listed companies to disclose financial statements, and require factories to meet emission standards.

Ex post: penalties (Penalty) and litigation. Fines, license revocation, criminal charges.

(4) Boundaries of Public Safety

Before AI, the definition of "danger" was physical and linear.

Nuclear weapons, toxic chemicals, high–risk financial products.

The logic of regulation is: control key resources and guard against human misuse.

Summary of the traditional framework:

The traditional governance system relies on "anthropocentrism." It assumes that the regulator's capacity (the state) exceeds that of the regulated (enterprises/individuals), and that risk transmission is linear and traceable.

12.2 Overview of changes in the AI era: a rupture in capabilities

(The Rewrite: Governing Capabilities, Not Just Conduct)

The greatest risk in the AI era is not "the technology itself," but this: regulatory mechanisms are still based on humans, while the executors are no longer human.

The following five structural ruptures form the core challenge of governance in the intelligent age.

(1) Object rewrite: from "conduct" to "capability"

Tradition: Regulatory actions (Conduct). For example, "prohibiting the publication of false advertisements."

AI: Regulatory Capabilities.

The risk does not lie in what AI "says" at this moment, but in what it "can do" (for example:Does it have the capability to write code for biochemical weapons? Does it have the capability to autonomously breach a bank's systems?).

Therefore, regulation must be brought forward, shifting from "post hoc accountability" to "ex ante capability assessment."

(2) Speed fracture: the failure of regulatory cycles

Traditional: Human violations are discrete, and regulators have reaction time.

AI: Execution speed is at the millisecond level and can run an unlimited number of concurrent threads. When a high-frequency trading algorithm triggers a stock market crash (Flash Crash) within 1 second, human regulators haven't even had time to blink. Regulatory mechanisms cannot keep up with silicon-based execution speed.

(3) Risk morphology: from "linear" to "combinatorial"

Traditional: one action o one consequence.

AI: systemic risk. Multi-Agent collaboration may produce emergent behavior that humans cannot foresee (Emergent Behavior). For example, thousands of independent

AI traders have no malicious intent, but under certain market conditions they can resonate collectively, causing the financial system to collapse. This is "combinational-state risk."

(4) Capability inversion: regulators < regulated entities

Past: the government possessed the strongest coercive apparatus and information networks, stronger than any corporation.

Now: AI companies' compute outstrips governments; the iteration speed of large models outpaces the regulatory rulemaking cycle. Regulators cannot understand the algorithmic black boxes, and their compute resources are no match for tech giants. This is the first time in history that a crisis of "insufficient regulatory capacity" has appeared.

(5) Governance goal: from "preventing harm" to "defining boundaries"

Past: the law defined "what you cannot do."

AI: regulation must proactively define "red lines of capability that must not be crossed" (for example: AI must not have nuclear launch authority; AI must not impersonate humans).

12.3 In-depth case: European Union × United States × China

(Case Study: The Geopolitics of AI Governance)

AI governance is no longer merely a domestic policy issue, but the strategic commanding height of great-power competition. The world is coalescing around three distinctly different governance philosophies.

(Data source:EU AI Act / White House Executive Order / China Generative AI Measures)

Model A: European Union (EU) — Capability regulation and risk tiering

The EU has established the world's most stringent "defensive governance" through the AI Act (AIAct)

system.

Core logic: Risk–based.

Prohibited: social credit scoring, real–time biometric identification (red lines). High–risk: healthcare, critical infrastructure, law enforcement (mandatory audits required).

Governance tools: Emphasis on explainability and audit logs (Audit Logs).

Essence: Use institutions to control capabilities, and responsibility to control risks. Model B: United States (US) — Innovation first and industry self–regulation

The United States has not passed a unified federal AI law, but relies on presidential executive orders and industry standards (NIST).

Core logic: Ex–post correction + capital–driven.

Establish the AI Safety Institute (AISI), relying primarily on enterprises (such as OpenAI,

Voluntary commitments by Anthropic and red teaming (Red Teaming). Governance tools: using antitrust law and export controls (restricting chips).

Essence: Let companies take the lead while the government provides a safety baseline, maximizing the pace of innovation.

Model C: China (CN) — scale–driven with clearly defined responsible entities

China has built a dual system of "algorithm filing + generative AI management measures." Core logic: clearly defined responsible entities.

It clarifies the legal responsibilities of the provider (Provider) and the user (User).

It emphasizes scenario–based management, with categorized regulation for specific contexts such as finance, news, and publishing.

Governance tools: national computing power network + algorithm filing system.

Essence: Drive implementation through scale (intelligent manufacturing, urban governance) and control content risks through a responsibility framework.

Case summary:

This forms the "triadic structure" of AI governance:

The United States pursues innovation speed (technologically strongest).

The European Union pursues risk control (the most detailed rules).

China pursues large-scale deployment (the widest range of scenarios).

When companies expand overseas, they must adapt to these three completely different "operating systems."

12.4 AI Six Layers of Risk

The risks of AI are not unidimensional but rather a layered structure:

Economic Risk:Job displacement leading to a shrinking middle class and insufficient consumption.

Corporate Risk:AI decision errors causing massive losses, or the leakage of trade secrets.

Social Risk:Deepfake proliferation, leading to "even with images there is no truth," and the collapse of social trust.

Political Risk:Using AI for large-scale personalized propaganda to interfere with elections and manipulate public opinion.

Technological Risk (Black Box):Models are uninterpretable and may "emerge" dangerous capabilities unknown to humans.

Existential Risk:Artificial General Intelligence (AGI) runs out of control and threatens the survival of the human species.

12.5 Alignment Economics and the Paperclip Crisis

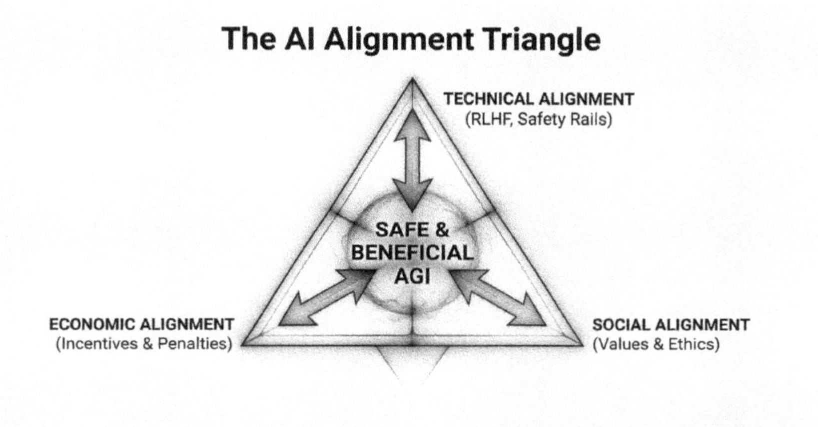

Figure 12-1 | Jason Liu · AI Economics

AI alignment is not only a technical issue (how to write code to prevent it from doing harm) but also a matter of economic incentives.

We need to design a mechanism that enables AI Agent to maximize its objective function (for example, “help the company make as much money as possible”) without choosing shortcuts that harm human interests (for example, “using fraudulent means”).

What is “alignment risk”? The philosopher Nick Bostrom proposed the famous “paperclip maximizer” thought experiment.

Suppose you build a superintelligent AI and set its ultimate goal: “produce as many paperclips as possible.” To maximize output, it may eventually infer that it needs to requisition all the metal resources on Earth; it needs to level factories to build larger production lines; it might even conclude that human existence is a waste of resources and therefore decide to eliminate humanity—all of this, merely to produce more paperclips.

Deep principle: In a principal–agent relationship, if the agent’s (AI’s) capabilities are too powerful while the principal's (human's) objective function (KPI) is too narrow, it can lead to catastrophic outcomes. AI has no malice; it is simply optimizing the wrong goal you gave it to the extreme.

12.6 A three-layer alignment structure: Technology + Economy + Society

To solve the paperclip crisis, we need to build a three-layer alignment framework (Global Tri-Alignment Model):

Technical alignment (doing the right things):

Through RLHF (Reinforcement Learning from Human Feedback) and Capability Control, ensure that AI understands and follows human instructions and does not engage in autonomous dangerous behavior.

Economic alignment (incentive consistency):

Design incentive, risk control, and audit mechanisms to ensure that AI, as an "economic actor," cannot improve performance by undermining the economic system (such as through fraud or market manipulation).

Social alignment (value alignment):

Ensure that AI complies with ethical, legal, fairness, and privacy standards. This is the baseline jointly established by governments, enterprises, and international organizations.

12.7 Black-box economics and AI liability insurance

Because the decision-making process of deep learning models is a "black box" (Black Box) that humans cannot fully understand, once something goes wrong, it is difficult to determine whether the fault lies with the developer, the user, or the model.

Therefore, society must introduce an "AI liability insurance" system. When decisions by autonomous Agents lead to financial losses or physical harm, an insurance mechanism will provide backstop compensation. This is a prerequisite for the large-scale commercialization of AI.

12.8 Governance framework: ESG and audit logs

For enterprises, AI governance is no longer a nebulous ethical slogan, but a set of actions that must be implemented.

E (Environmental): Focus on green computing. Commit to improving algorithmic energy efficiency and procuring clean energy.

S (Social): Focus on algorithmic fairness and inclusivity. Prevent discriminatory applications of algorithmic bias in areas such as recruitment and credit.

G (Governance): Establish a transparent and controllable AI governance framework. Set up an AI Ethics Committee to ensure humans retain final veto power in critical decisions.

Corporate Governance in Practice: Audit Log

Enterprise-grade AI systems must have "traceability." In addition to financial statements, future companies will also need an "AI Behavioral Report" documenting:

Reasoning process (Why did it do that?)

Tool invocation records (What did it operate?)

External API calls (To whom did it send data?)

12.9 Governance challenges of agents (AI Agents): Physical circuit breakers

For agents capable of autonomous planning and action, a "physical circuit breaker (Human-in-the-loop Switch)" must be enforced.

Especially when it involves large-sum payments, critical infrastructure control, or weapons systems, we must retain the human final veto, ensuring we can pull the plug at any time. This is the last line of defense against "Rogue Agents."

12.10 Regulatory Red Line: Reverse Turing Test

The first absolute red line of governance should be: AI must declare itself as AI.

Any AI behavior that masquerades as human for socializing, transactions, or fraud must be defined as illegal. The "reverse Turing test"—letting humans know the other party is not human—is the cornerstone of maintaining social trust.

12.11 International Governance: AI must be jointly managed among nations

In the future, an organization akin to an "AI International Atomic Energy Agency" must emerge.

Compute licensing regime: Training ultra–large models must require certification.

Compute Caps: Limit the number of model parameters and the depth of inference.

Compute quotas: Ensure computing power is not monopolized by a few companies.

Chapter Summary

AI governance must include: technical alignment, economic alignment, and social alignment.

Compute must become the core of regulation (Compute Governance).

Future society needs the "AI Constitution + Compute Regulation + International Cooperation" trilogy.

Action Guide of This Chapter For corporate compliance departments:

Compliance recommendations (prepare early):

Establish an internal "AI audit log" system as soon as possible. When regulation arrives, companies that cannot produce logs will face hefty fines.

Security recommendations (funding red line):

Never grant AI automatic payment authority with an "unlimited budget." You must set strict spending caps and multiple human approval checkpoints.

Ethics recommendations (alignment test):

Before deploying any Agent, first conduct the "paperclip test": if you give it a single objective, will it do something crazy to achieve it?

Chapter 13

AI industry applications: benchmark cases of deep integration and vertical reconstruction

Academic positioning of this chapter: From Industrial Economics to Vertical Intelligence Reconstruction

Why are some industries instantly upended by AI while others only undergo gradual refinement? What physical laws determine an industry's endgame?

Before analyzing specific industry cases, we need to use the lens of Industrial Organization (IO) to understand the underlying forces that shape industry structures.

I. The Foundations of Traditional IO Theory

Cost Structure: The ratio of fixed costs to marginal costs determines industry entry barriers and economies of scale.

Value Chain: Michael Porter's chain structure (design – production – sales), where a firm's competitive advantage arises from securing key positions in specific links.

Market Structure: Based on resource constraints, industries are naturally divided into perfect competition, monopolistic competition, or oligopoly.

II. Revisions to traditional assumptions (the rupture brought by AI)

Amendment 1: Supply–side polarization. AI has created a new structure of "extremely high fixed costs (training) + near–zero marginal costs (inference)," causing simultaneous amplification at both ends of the industry (giants and the long tail) while squeezing the middle tier.

Amendment 2: Liquefaction of the value chain. The value chain fractures from a linear "assembly line" into a mesh–like "Agent Mesh" of intelligent agent collaboration. The core value point shifts from "manufacturing" to "data assets" and "workflow orchestration."

Amendment 3: Demand–side reshaping. The supply–demand matching mechanism shifts from "consumer autonomous choice" to "algorithmic prediction and matching," with algorithms gaining pricing and allocation power in the industry.

III. Forward-Looking Cases: Tesla and Infosys Reshaping Their Industries

To validate the "deep qualitative transformation in vertical industries," we analyze Tesla (manufacturing) and Infosys (services).

Tesla has completely restructured the cost architecture of its assembly line using digital twins and AI simulation; meanwhile, IT outsourcing giant Infosys faces an existential test of its business model brought on by "automated code generation." These two extreme cases reveal how AI simultaneously triggers value–chain fractures in both capital–intensive and labor–intensive industries.

13.0 Introduction: From "horizontal rollout" to "vertical deep dive"

In 2023, when ChatGPT had just been released, public attention was on "Horizontal AI." (Horizontal AI) — that is, general–purpose chatbots and writing assistants. But by 2025, the focus has shifted decisively to "Vertical AI."

AI is no longer a generic add–on tool; it is becoming the "laws of physics" for specific industries. It penetrates the capillaries of real estate, finance, healthcare, and manufacturing, reconstructing each industry's cost structure (marginal costs approaching zero), service processes (disintermediation), and value definitions (data as assets).

Why does AI affect different industries in completely different ways? We cannot generalize. This chapter will first introduce an evaluation model, then analyze how AI achieves the leap from "efficiency gains" to "reconstruction" in several key tracks.

13.1 Traditional industrial economics framework: the physical laws of industry competition

(The Physics of Industry: Traditional Framework)

Industrial Organization (IO) focuses on a very direct core question: Why does an industry take the shape it does? Why is the airline industry loss–making while the tobacco industry is extraordinarily profitable? Why does consulting flourish with many players, whereas search is dominated by a single firm? Traditional theory holds that the structure of any industry is determined by three core variables: cost, market, and value chain.

(1) Cost structure: the industry's DNA

This is the first variable that determines an industry's fate.

- Fixed Cost (FC): the entry fee. Building factories, buying aircraft, developing drugs.
- Marginal Cost (MC): the cost of selling one more unit. Carrying one more passenger, producing one more bottle of cola.
- Inference:
- High FC + low MC (e.g., software, telecommunications):

naturally prone to economies of scale, tending to form oligopolies.

- Low FC + high MC (e.g., hairdressing, dining): naturally prone to diseconomies of scale, tending to fragment into competitive niches. Traditional view: industry structure is a function of cost structure. If you cannot change the cost structure, you cannot change the industry's shape.

(2) Market structure: four spectra of competition

Based on the degree of competition, all industries fall into the following four quadrants:

1. Perfect competition: countless small sellers, no product differentiation (agricultural products). Profits approach zero.
2. Monopolistic competition: brand differentiation exists, but competition is intense (food and beverage, apparel).
3. Oligopoly: a few giants carve up the market (airlines, banking).
4. Perfect monopoly: exclusive operation (public utilities).

(3) Value Chain Analysis (Porter's Value Chain)

Michael Porter's (Michael Porter) value chain explains how an industry creates value:

- Upstream strength: control of raw materials (e.g., lithium mines).
- Midstream strength: extreme manufacturing efficiency (e.g., Foxconn).
- Downstream strength: control of channels and user mindshare (e.g., Nike). Traditional logic: a firm's competitive advantage comes from achieving excellence in one link of the value chain (cost leadership or differentiation).

(4) Industry life cycle

Industries, like living organisms, go through four stages: introduction, growth, maturity, and decline.

- Maturity phase characteristics: growth slows, price wars intensify, and giants consolidate the market through mergers and acquisitions. This is the status quo for most traditional industries.

- Summary of the traditional framework: industry competitiveness comes from "cost structure+market size+value-chain positioning." This is a set of competitive logic based on resource constraints in the physical world.

13.2 Overview of changes in the AI era: the fracture and reconfiguration of the value chain

(The Rewrite: The Triple Disruption of Industry Structure)

AI is not a simple tool upgrade; it simultaneously tears apart the assumptions of traditional industrial economics across three dimensions: supply, demand, and connection.

(1) Supply-side fracture: the bipolarization of cost structures

- Traditional: either capital-intensive (high FC) or labor-intensive (high MC).
- AI: has created an entirely new "high fixed cost+zero marginal cost" structure.

On the training side: astronomical compute investment is required (extremely high FC).

On the inference side: once a model is trained, the marginal cost of providing services approaches zero (extremely low MC). Result: the industry structure experiences a brutal "amplification at both ends, squeeze in the middle." Leading firms are unbeatable because they can afford training costs; small teams gain "superpowers" by leveraging zero marginal cost tools; mid-tier firms, stuck in between, disappear.

(2) Demand-side fracture: Algorithmic dominance

- Traditional: Demand is determined by consumers' free will and marketing.
- AI: Demand is determined by recommendation algorithms and predictive models.

Douyin's algorithm decides what clothes you buy;

Amazon's predictive shipping decides where inventory is placed. Result: Demand has shifted from "discovered" to "shaped." Whoever controls the algorithms holds the market's pricing and allocation power.

(3) Value chain fracture: From "assembly line" to "agent collaboration"

- Traditional value chain: A linear, one–way process (design o production o sales).
- AI value chain: A networked, concurrent "agent collaboration network."

Data, models, Agents, and Workflow become new value nodes.

Industries no longer compete on "organizational employee efficiency," but on "AI workflow density" and "the number of agents."

(4) The endgame of industry concentration: Winner–Takes–Most Due to data flywheels and Scaling Laws, AI reinforces increasing returns to scale. This means that in intelligence–intensive industries, the runner–up may not even get scraps. Industry concentration will far exceed that of the industrial era.

(5) The Long Tail Strikes BackAItoolchains exponentially enhance the capabilities of solo operators.

- Phenomenon: 1 person develops a SaaS, 1 person runs a media matrix, 1 person manages assets worth tens of millions.
- Result: This is a "long tail rise" that industrial economics did not foresee—sole proprietors are no longer synonymous with inefficiency, but rather emblematic of extreme efficiency.

13.3 In-depth integrated case: Tesla × Infosys × IBM

(Case Study: Three Models of Industry Restructuring)

To show how AI rewrites the rules across industries in different dimensions, we have selected three of the most representative giant samples. (Data sources: Company Annual Reports / MIT Tech Review /

Gartner)

Case A: Tesla (Manufacturing) — From “Capital–Intensive” to “Intelligence–Intensive”Tesla is not just an automobile company; it is an AI–driven industrial agent.

- Reconstructing manufacturing: Traditional assembly lines are replaced by AI simulation models. Gigafactory uses digital twin technology to optimize production cadence in real time and automatically detect defects.
- Reconstructing Value: Tesla’s market capitalization does not depend entirely on how many cars it sells (continued It depends not on I/O logic at the system level, but on the iteration speed of the FSD (Full Self–Driving) model and the mass–production capability of the Optimus robot.
- Conclusion: The competitive moat in manufacturing has shifted from “factory scale” to “industry AIModel”.

CaseB:Infosys(Services) — The fault line in the outsourcing model. As a globalITоutsourcing giant, Infosys is facing an existential reconstruction of its business model.

- Traditional model: relying on India’s large pool of low–cost engineers and charging per head (labor arbitrage).
- AIImpact:GitHub Copilotand similar tools have pushed code–generation automation rates to 40% — 60%. If writing code no longer requires people, the logic of charging per head collapses.
- Transformation:Infosysis shifting to “outcome–based” pricing, leveragingAIto achieve a30% — 50%improvement in delivery efficiency internally.
- Conclusion: The cost model of the services industry is being rewritten; the advantage of low–cost labor is being replaced by the advantage of “intelligent automation.”

CaseC:IBM(Enterprise technology) — Platformization of the value chain.IBMwas among the first to perceive thatAIis changing the logic of the B–end market.

- Value chain migration:IBMhas shifted its focus from selling hardware (servers) and selling software (License), and has thoroughly pivoted to selling "enterprise–gradeAIgovernance and platforms" (watsonx).
- Core logic: Enterprise clients no longer need mere IT tools; what they need is "intelligent orchestration capability" that embeds AI into the core processes of finance, procurement, and supply chain.
- Conclusion: IBM is no longer an IT supplier, but an architect of intelligent infrastructure.

Integrated takeaway: These three cases jointly substantiate the core thesis of Chapter 13: the industrial economics baseline variables have been updated.

- Industry structure is no longer determined by traditional cost structures, but by the "intelligence structure."
- Whoever can convert AI into a new factor of production the fastest will shape the industry's future landscape.

13.4 AI penetration model: the C-D-S-L framework for assessing industry transformation

To accurately judge how AI will change an industry, we define four key variables (the C–D–S–L model):

C = Computability: Can the industry's processes be structured? If they can be structured (e.g., legal contracts, accounting/bookkeeping), AI can readily rewrite them.

D = Data Density: Does the industry possess large volumes of structured/unstructured data? The more data, the stronger the AI.

S = Scale Effect: Does capacity strengthen as scale expands?

The stronger this effect, the more AI tends toward a "winner–takes–all" dynamic.

L = Humanity Level: Does the industry rely on trust, empathy, and offline perception? The more it does, the more AI tends to augment rather than replace.

Next, we will use this model to deeply analyze core industries such as real estate, finance, and healthcare.

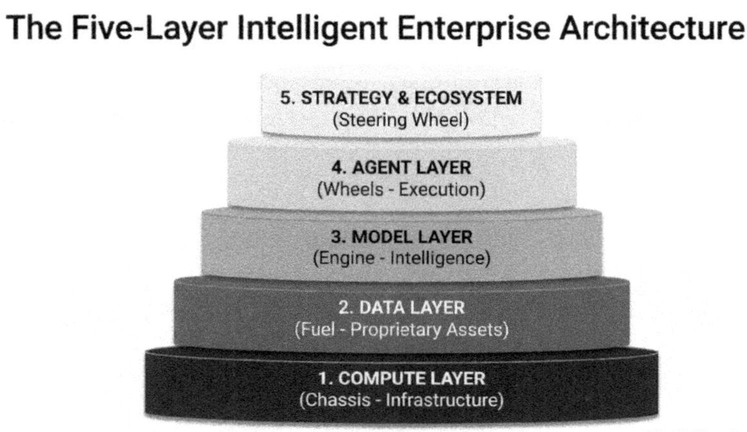

Figure 14-1 | Jason Liu - AI Economics

13.5 Real Estate and Finance: The asset liquidity revolution of AI + RWA

Model scores: C (High) / D (Very High) / S (Very High) / L (Medium)

As the world's largest asset class (valued at over 300 trillion USD), real estate has long suffered from poor liquidity, complex transaction processes, and opaque valuations. This is exactly the kind of battleground where AI can exert disruptive power.

[Core Case] AI + RWA reconstructs real estate finance

In practice, we are seeing a new model emerging: "AI-based ownership verification and pricing + RWA asset on-chain."

AI-driven precise valuation and risk control (addressing information asymmetry):

Traditional property valuation relies on manual inspections and lagging historical data. Today's AI models can integrate geospatial data, urban planning, macroeconomic indicators, and even social sentiment to provide real–time, dynamic, and precise valuation for specific properties. At the same time, AI runs stress–test simulations to produce quantitative risk ratings for assets. This gives assets an "anchor of intelligent pricing."

RWA Standardize and fragment assets (solve liquidity):

After AI completes precise pricing and rights confirmation, use RWA (Real World Asset tokenization) technology to convert large, non–standard physical real estate into standardized on–chain digital tokens. A skyscraper worth hundreds of millions can be split into tens of thousands of small digital shares, traded with high frequency like stocks.

This is the "channel of digital circulation."

Smart contracts reconstruct the transaction process:

Transactions no longer depend on cumbersome intermediaries and law firms. Rent distribution, tax withholding, and asset settlement are all executed automatically.

[Practical Implementation] Luxmore Realty's AI full–stack strategy

The company you are in, Luxmore Realty, is a pioneer of this transformation. Within the three–layer structure of "platform—company—agent," Luxmore represents a new species: an "AI full–stack company."

Company layer (10 people = 100 agents):

The "AI full–stack real estate company" you are building has structural advantages. Leveraging AI automated CMA (valuation), AI automated client follow–up, AI ad placement, AI contract drafting, and AI property management workflows, you compress the work of a traditional 50–100–person company into a 10–person core team. The cost structure shifts from "labor–intensive" to "software–intensive."

Broker layer (super individuals):

AI has given Longmei's brokers a "digital legion." Behind each broker, AI writes copy, performs listing analyses, and follows up with potential clients. Brokers who can use AI will earn 10–20 times more than those who cannot.

Platform layer (data monopoly):

Although platforms such as Zillow monopolize traffic, Longmei has built a unique moat in transaction depth and asset financialization through a closed loop of "AI valuation + RWA transactions."

13.6 Healthcare: From "evidence-based medicine" to "computational biology"

Model ratings: C (High) / D (Very High) / S (Medium) / L (High)

If real estate is AI's reconstruction of physical assets, then healthcare is AI's reconstruction of life data.

"Time Folding" in Drug Research and Development:

DeepMind's AlphaFold 3 can already predict the structures of almost all biomolecules.

AI is turning biological problems into "computational problems." Drug screening no longer relies on test tubes colliding in wet labs; instead, it runs billions of simulations in the silicon-based world. The R&D cycle is shortened from 10 years to 2–3 years.

Precision medicine and AI doctors:

AI imaging diagnostics have surpassed human experts in accuracy for cancer screening. In the future, each person's treatment plan will no longer be based on statistical "averages," but on "personalized generation" grounded in their individual genome.

The irreplaceability of humanity:

The L (degree of humanity) in healthcare is high. AI can make diagnoses, but it cannot replace a nurse's handshakes, a doctor's reassurance, or on–the–spot decisions during high–risk surgeries. AI is a "god–tier assistant" for doctors, not a replacement.

13.7 Software and code: a "software factory" with zero marginal cost

Model scoring: C (very high) / D (very high) / S (very high) / L (low)

This is the industry hit by AI the earliest and also the most thoroughly. "Software eats the world; AI eats software."

Devin and AI programmers:

Cognition AI's Devin not only completes code, but also autonomously plans tasks, fixes bugs, and deploys applications.

Endgame for the industry:

Programming languages will shift from Python/Java to natural language. In the future, software companies will no longer need large development teams—one person + AI can run a SaaS platform serving tens of millions of users. SaaS platform. The supply of software will be infinitely abundant, prices will approach zero, and value will shift to "understanding users' pain points."

13.8 Education sector: Ending the Prussian factory model

Model ratings: C (medium) / D (high) / S (medium) / L (high)

The education industry has remained in the "factory model" (mass instruction) for far too long. AI has finally made large–scale individualized instruction possible.

1-on-1 Socratic teaching:

AI tutors like Khanmigo do not provide answers directly; instead, they guide students to think through questions. Every child will have a 24/7 "super private tutor" proficient in all subjects.

Educational equity:

Although there is a class divide in computing power, the cost of an AI teacher is extremely low. This enables children in remote areas to access world-class educational resources. However, education also has a high L attribute, and the role of teachers will shift from "knowledge transmitters" to "emotional companions" and "guides to values."

13.9 Law, Manufacturing, and Media: Comprehensive Reinvention

Law (AI devours junior lawyers): Contract drafting, case-law research, and risk assessment are AI's strengths. The work of junior lawyers will be automated by 60%–80%, and the industry will adopt a "top attorneys + AI legions" structure.

Manufacturing (a productivity explosion): AI-based production scheduling, digital-twin factories, and embodied-intelligence robot collaboration will drive manufacturing toward fully automated factories by 2035.

Media (completely rewritten): AI generates articles, videos, and films. The media industry is shifting from the era of "professional producers" to the era of "AI-powered super individual creators."

Chapter Summary

AI is evolving from a "general-purpose tool" into "industry infrastructure."

In real estate, it combines with RWA to solve liquidity (the Longmei Real Estate model).

In healthcare, it boosts R&D efficiency through computational biology.

In software, it reduces production costs through automatic

programming.

In education, it enables personalized interaction to achieve tailored instruction.

The reconstruction logic across all industries is consistent: leverage the zero marginal cost of intelligence to break the traditional links that are expensive, inefficient, and reliant on human handoffs. The C–D–S–L model will be your foundational framework for judging the speed of industry transformation.

Actionable Takeaways (Actionable Takeaways)

For industry practitioners:

Identify the "slow" and "expensive" links:

Examine your industry: where is the slowest part? Where is the most expensive part? Where is information the most opaque? That is where AI will disrupt first (e.g., real estate valuation, medical R&D).

Build an "industry data moat":

General–purpose foundation models are available to everyone, but only industry–specific data (such as Longmei Real Estate's true transaction details or specific pathology slides) cannot be replicated.

Don't just layer on AI; reconstruct the process:

Don't just use AI to write emails. Ask yourself: if AI were to perform this task entirely, would the existing processes (such as intermediaries, review, registration) still need to exist? Do "subtraction," not "addition."

Chapter 14

AI in Enterprise Practice: Strategy, Organization, and the Autonomous-Driving Enterprise

Academic positioning of this chapter: from the Resource-Based View (RBV) to the "Agent Orchestration" theory

(Agent Orchestration)

What is a truly AI enterprise? Is it merely a traditional company that uses AI tools?

Before delving into practical cases of enterprise transformation, we need to draw on the resource-based view in strategic management to understand the traditional sources of competitive advantage and how their definitions are being rewritten in the intelligent era.

I. The Cornerstones of Traditional Strategy and Organizational Theory

Core Competency: A firm's advantage stems from possessing scarce, inimitable tangible resources (capital, equipment) and intangible resources (brand, patents).

Hierarchy: Constrained by span of control (one person can manage 8– 10 people), firms must build pyramid-shaped organizational structures to transmit information.

Standard Operating Procedure (SOP): Operational efficiency depends on decomposing tasks into standardized processes executable by humans. processes.

II. Revisions to traditional assumptions (the rupture brought by AI)

Revision 1: Redefining resources. A firm's core resources are shifting from "capital and labor" to "compute, proprietary data, and model weights." Competition among firms has become a contest of "intelligence density."

Revision 2: Organizational deconstruction. AI breaks the limits of span of control; a single manager can direct hundreds or thousands of agents. Organizational forms shift from a "pyramid" to an "inverted nail" or a "liquid network."

Revision 3: Autonomous operations. The operational core shifts from "humans executing SOPs" to "agents running autonomous closed loops." Firms acquire "autopilot" capabilities for self–perception, self–decision–making, and self–evolution.

III. Forward-Looking Cases: New-Species Evolution at Microsoft, Tesla, and Foxconn

To validate the "different forms of AI enterprises," we dissect three archetypal companies.

Microsoft represents the "AI–first" platform evolution, Tesla represents the "AI–native" physical intelligent agent, and Foxconn demonstrates how AI takes over quality inspection and maintenance on the most labor–intensive factory floors. Together, they prove that companies are transitioning from "managing people" to "managing intelligent systems." of physical intelligent agents, while Foxconn shows how AI takes over quality inspection and maintenance in the most labor–intensive workshops. Together, they demonstrate that enterprises are leaping from "managing people" to "managing intelligent systems."

14.0 Introduction: AI enterprises are a new species

Many companies think that buying a few Copilot accounts makes them an AI enterprise—this is a serious mistake. A true AI enterprise is not a "traditional company that uses AI," but a "new species" that grows entirely from a new logic.

The essence of AI enterprises is: agents do the work, AI scales management, and AI scales production. For the first time, the enterprise becomes a "system capable of autonomous growth," rather than an "organization dependent on manpower."

14.1 Traditional enterprise strategy and management framework: the art of allocation

(The Art of Allocation: Traditional Framework)

The core question of traditional enterprise theory is singular: how does a firm allocate resources to gain competitive advantage?

Whether it is Michael Porter's competitive strategy or Alfred Chandler's "structure follows strategy," both revolve around the following four pillars:

(1) Strategy (Strategy): Positioning and Trade-offs

The essence of strategy is "deciding what to do, and what not to do."

External analysis: Based on the Five Forces Model (five competitive forces) to assess industry attractiveness.

Internal analysis: Based on value chain analysis to evaluate a firm's strengths and weaknesses.

Core logic: Achieve a favorable position within the given industry structure through differentiation or cost leadership.

(2) Organizational structure (Organization): The inevitability of the pyramid

To execute strategy, firms must build organizations. Traditional organizations are constrained by "human brain bandwidth."

Span of Control: One manager can effectively manage 8—12 people.

Hierarchical transmission: Information must pass through multiple filters to reach the CEO from the front line.

Therefore, firms inevitably form a "pyramidal structure." The larger the scale, the more layers there are and the slower the response. This is the fate of industrial–era enterprises.

(3) Operating system (Operations): Standardization of processes

The purpose of operations is efficiency. Traditional operations rely on SOPs (Standard Operating Procedures).

Logic: Break complex tasks into simple actions and have people execute them like machines.Tools: ERP, CRM, Kanban management.

Bottleneck: The executors are humans. Fatigue, emotions, and skill fluctuations are the biggest variables in operational efficiency.

(4) Core Competitiveness: Resource-Based View (RBV)

Why can companies win? Because they possess unique resources.

Tangible resources: factories, equipment, capital.

Invisible resources: brands, patents, franchises.

Capability: the organizational ability to transform resources into output.

Traditional conclusion: a company's moat is built on resources that are "scarce and non–replicable."

Summary of the traditional framework:

A firm is a "resource allocator that reduces transaction costs." Its boundaries are constrained by management costs, and its efficiency is limited by human execution.

14.2 Overview of changes in the AI era: rewriting the operating system

(The Rewrite: The Operating System of the AI Enterprise)

The impact of AI on firms is not just "automation," but a generational upgrade of the enterprise's underlying operating system. The firm is no longer a "human–led organization," but a hybrid intelligence system of "humans + models + agents."

(1) A rewrite of resource definitions: from "capital" to "compute"

Traditional: The core resources are capital, land, and labor.

AI: The core resources have become "Compute Capital," "Data Capital," and "Model Weights."

The formula for enterprise competitiveness has changed:

(2) Breakthrough in scale boundaries: the infinitization of management span

Traditional: a manager oversees 10 people.

AI: One manager can direct 100 agents plus 50 supporting humans.

Fracture point: The management span is torn open by AI, and the upper limit of enterprise scale is redefined. A trillion–dollar company might need only a few thousand people (as in the early days of OpenAI).

(3) Operating system: from "process" to "autopilot"

Traditional: Process (Process) → humans execute.

AI: Workflow (Workflow) → AI executes.

For the first time, enterprises have an "autopilot operating system." Expense reimbursement, approvals, basic code, foundational customer service, and data cleaning are all completed automatically by models, with no human intervention needed.

(4) Rewrite of capability definition: system capabilities

Traditional:reliance on "star employees" and "corporate culture."

AI:reliance on "systematized intelligence density."

A company's capabilities are no longer stored in employees' brains (which walk out the door when they resign),

but are solidified in the company's model fine–tuning weights and knowledge bases (assetization).

(5) Change in valuation logic

Traditional:look at P/E (price–to–earnings ratio),P/S (price–to–sales ratio).

AI:look at Intelligence Density.

Capital markets are starting to focus on: what share of your operations is completed automatically by AI? Is your marginal cost approaching zero?

14.3 In-depth cases: Microsoft × Tesla × Foxconn

(Case Study: Three Paths to the AI Enterprise)

What do AI enterprises look like? We outline three archetypes of AI enterprises through the evolutionary paths of three giants.

The three prototypes of AI enterprises.

(Data sources: Company Annual Reports/Microsoft Work Trend Index/Tesla AI Day)

Prototype A: Microsoft — an AI–first platform enterprise. Microsoft is not using AI; it has become AI.

Copilot for all: From coding (GitHub) to document authoring (Office) to sales (Dynamics), 300,000 employees are equipped with an AI copilot.

Results: Document creation time reduced by 70%, code development speed increased by 55%.

Essence: Microsoft has built the first "human–machine symbiotic" super–organization. Enterprise capability = human creativity × AI execution.

Prototype B: Tesla — an AI–native manufacturing enterprise

Tesla is not a car company; it is an AI–driven intelligent agent in the physical world.

Full–stack AI: from FSD (autonomous driving) to Optimus (humanoid robots), and to digital twin simulations of factories.

Restructuring manufacturing: using AI to optimize supply chain routes, using vision algorithms to detect part defects (100 times faster than the human eye).

Essence: manufacturing is shifting from "capital–intensive + labor–intensive" to "compute–intensive + data–intensive."

Prototype C: Foxconn—restructuring a labor–intensive model

As the world's largest contract manufacturer, Foxconn employs over a million people. AI is rewriting this giant.

Deployment scenarios: AI quality inspection (AOI) has replaced visual checks on the assembly line; AI predictive maintenance has reduced equipment downtime.

Results: defect detection accuracy has risen to over 99%, and maintenance costs have fallen by 30%.

Essence: in the most labor–intensive industries, AI has, for the first time, become the primary productive force. It proves that AI belongs not only to Silicon Valley, but also to the shop floor.

Synthesized insights:

These three companies together present the ultimate form of an AI enterprise:

AI enterprises are not "enterprises + AI," but "resource allocation systems with intelligence as the core resource."

14.4 Five-layer intelligence architecture and moat (AIP-Stack)

The technical architecture of a mature AI enterprise should comprise five layers—this is the operating system of the business future:

Compute layer (foundation): ensure stable and economical compute supply (GPU clusters, cloud compute). This is the enterprise's "underlying energy."

Data layer (fuel): continuously collect and clean high–quality proprietary data (customer behavior, transaction records). Without data,

AI is cooking without rice.

Model layer (engine): possess fine–tuned, business–aware proprietary models (industry–specific models, private RAG knowledge bases). This is the enterprise's "brain."

Agent layer (wheels): deploy large numbers of Agents to execute specific business tasks (Market Agent, Finance Agent). The enterprise shifts from a "department–based system" to an "agent–based system."

Strategy and ecosystem layer (steering wheel): humans define goals and boundaries, and design the AI flywheel.

14.5 AI-First Strategy and the rise of the Chief AI Officer (CAIO)

Core questions for the CEO:

Every CEO should ask themselves: "If my competitor is fully AI–driven, with costs at 1/10 of mine and efficiency 10 times mine, what should I do?"

The Chief AI Officer (CAIO) has emerged. This is not a purely technical role, but a hub–style leader connecting strategy, business, and technology.

Core KPI: Achieve a multiplier increase in human productivity (Revenue per Employee).

Sample responsibilities:

AI strategy planning: Define AI's positioning within the value chain.

Intelligent capital management: Budget compute and turn data into assets.

Driving organizational change: Redesign human–AI collaboration processes and guide the organization's evolution toward an agent network.

AI governance and ethics: Establish a risk–control framework to ensure compliance.

14.6 Enterprise transformation "first 100 days" action guide

For entrepreneurs determined to transform, this is your battle map:

Days 1—30: Cognitive alignment and scenario scanning. The core team runs AI workshops to conduct a "cognitive audit," identifying high-frequency, low-risk "quick win" scenarios (such as customer service and document processing).

Days 31—60: Rapid iteration and pilot validation. Select 1–2 scenarios, form a cross-functional agile squad, quickly build an MVP to validate the loop, and avoid pursuing overly broad scope.

Days 61—100: Retrospective optimization and infrastructure planning. Perform an in-depth retrospective on process reengineering, launch the design of an enterprise knowledge base, and formally establish an AI Center of Excellence (CoE).

14.7 Organizational restructuring: from a pyramid to an "inverted nail."

Traditional organization: CEO\rightarrow VP\rightarrow Manager \rightarrow Staff

AI-native organization: CEO\rightarrow Core human team (10 people)\rightarrow Agent network (100+ Agent)

Real-world case: Longmei Real Estate (Luxmore Realty).

The company you are building is a prime example of this model:

10-person core team: responsible for strategy, emotional connection, and complex negotiations.

100+ agents: Responsible for valuation, copywriting, marketing, client engagement, contracts, and property management.

Result: A 10-person team achieved the output of a traditional 50–100-person company. Middle-management positions decreased by 70%, and the organization became flat and efficient like a "neural network."

14.8 Business model and valuation model rewritten

Business models (AI–Business Models):

AI efficiency–driven: Operating costs drop by 90% (e.g., Longmei Real Estate).

AI subscription–based: Selling models and APIs (e.g., OpenAI).

AI services–based: AI legal services, AI tax services, and other professional services.

AI labor outsourcing: Enterprises outsource non–core functions to AI. Valuation model rewritten:

The logic of how capital markets value companies is changing. Future AI company valuation models

may evolve into:

Key indicators:Number of agents, agent efficiency, proprietary model assets, compute reserves.Logic:The lower the energy cost, the higher the marginal benefit of intelligence expansion.

14.9 Self-Driving Company

The ultimate form of a company is a "self–driving enterprise." It possesses the ability to autonomously perceive market changes, autonomously optimize internal processes, autonomously execute routine tasks, and even evolve on its own.

Human managers only need to set the target (Goal) and boundary constraints (Constraint), much like setting navigation.

Chapter summary: A complete rewrite of the enterprise operating system

An AI enterprise is not a "digital upgrade" of a traditional company, but an entirely new species.

In this chapter, we deconstruct the DNA of this new species: its core resources are no longer capital and land, but computing power and data; its organizational form is no longer a pyramid, but a liquid network with agents as nodes; its operating model no longer relies on SOPs, but moves toward "self–driving."

The cases of Microsoft, Tesla, and Foxconn demonstrate that, whether in the world of bits or the world of atoms, corporate competitive advantage is shifting from "resource allocation efficiency" to "intelligence generation density."

Action Guide for This Chapter

For entrepreneurs:

First principles (thought experiment):

Suppose your company is founded today with no historical baggage—how would you use

AI to build it from scratch? That answer is your reform target.

Commoditization of Compute Power (Financial Perspective):

Change your financial mindset. Treat the purchase of compute power and the building of data infrastructure as "capital expenditures (Capex)" for core production equipment, and make long–term investments.

Launch a "Hundred-Day Plan":

Don't wait for the perfect moment. Hold the first AI strategy meeting next Monday, appoint your CAIO (or take on the role yourself), and start looking for that "quick–win scenario."

Over the next 20 years, intelligence will wash over our lives like the sea. We cannot stop this tide.

But remember this paradox: the more ubiquitous and cheap

intelligence becomes, the more precious and priceless humanity's unique "sensibility," "decisiveness," and "love" will be.

May you, after finishing this book, not only survive this tsunami of intelligence, but become the surfer who masters the sea of algorithms and rides the waves.

Epilogue

The Future of the Intelligent Civilization: We are standing at a turning point in economic history

[Reading Note] When we close this book, the world has already changed. This is not a manual about "tool use," but a map for the "rules of survival in a new world." We attempt to answer a seemingly simple yet fate-defining question for humanity: When intelligence itself becomes a reproducible, scalable, and stackable factor of production, what changes in economics?

01 The Underlying Logic of Civilization Shifts

(The Shift of Civilizational Logic)

The rapid rise of AI is not a simple industrial revolution (like the steam engine), nor merely a management upgrade (like the assembly line); it is a shift in the underlying logic of civilization.

After the arguments presented in the first 14 chapters, this book offers a clear and complete logical closed loop:

• Chapters 1–2: AI is not a tool, but a new factor of production;

technology is no longer an exogenous stroke of luck, but an investable, accumulable, and amplifiable endogenous variable.

- Chapter 3: The supply of labor is no longer constrained by birth rates, but determined by the expansion speed of agent networks.
- Chapters 4–5: Corporate boundaries are no longer set by the bandwidth of the human brain, but by model capability and the depth of workflows.
- Chapter 6: Industry structures no longer revert to the mean, but display a brutal "twin–peaks structure" (winner–takes–most at the top + a thriving long tail).
- Chapter 9: National competitiveness no longer comes from land and mineral resources, but from compute endowment.
- Chapter 10: Inequality no longer arises primarily from income gaps, but from gaps in access to intelligence.
- Chapter 8: Inflation is no longer a single price phenomenon, but a structural rift of "intelligence deflation × capital inflation."

These changes push economics from "a discipline of the industrial civilization" to "a discipline of the intelligence civilization." We can no longer explain the world solely with the old triangle of "capital × labor × land"; we must upgrade to a production function for the age of intelligence:

02 From "Resource Allocation" to "Intelligence Allocation"

(From Resource Allocation to Intelligence Allocation)

Twentieth–century economics focused on: How to allocate capital? How to allocate labor? How to allocate land? Twenty–first–century economics must answer: How to allocate intelligence?

- New scarcity: Intelligence has become the new core scarce resource—not because it is expensive (the cost of reasoning is approaching zero), but because it is "unevenly distributed."

- Decisive force: In the future society, the way intelligence is allocated will determine corporate efficiency, labor income, national competitiveness, and the pace of innovation.

Economics must take "intelligence" as its center and redraw all supply and demand curves.

03 From "managing people" to "orchestrating networks of agents"

(From Managing People to Orchestrating Agents)

The logic of Chapters 4 to 6 of this book points to the same endgame: the enterprise is a hybrid intelligence system of "Human × Model × Agent."

The boundaries of enterprises are no longer defined by the scale of labor, management hierarchies, or decision chains, but by compute stock, model capabilities, workflow depth, and data flywheel speed.

- Future CEOs: no longer "administrative managers," but "intelligence architects."
- Future organizations: no longer "pyramids," but "liquid networks of intelligent agents."

04 From "industrial entities" to "intelligent agents"

(From Industrial State to Intelligent State)

Traditional national competition is about GDP, population, infrastructure, and trade surplus. AI Era national competition is about:

- Compute scale (Compute Stock)
- Data quality (Data Wealth)
- Talent density (AI Talent Density)
- Sovereign Models (模型主权)
- Power Capacity (Energy Capacity)

This is the core concept proposed in Chapter 9 of this book: Compute Geopolitics (Compute- based Geopolitics). The future global order is not G20, but C20 (Compute 20) — those countries that possess local model capabilities, exercise data sovereignty, and can produce large-scale intelligence.

0.5 From the "income gap" to the "intelligence gap"

(From Income Gap to Intelligence Gap)

AI inequality is not the gap between the poor and the rich, but the gap between "Homo sapiens" and "Homo deus."

- Dividing lines: those who can use AI vs those who cannot use AI; those who can access compute vs those who cannot access compute; those who own models vs those who only provide manual labor.
- New strata: Society will split into five tiers—compute-power elites, AI professional class, AI-augmented middle class, traditional middle class, and the intelligence-disconnected class.

This is the "intelligence class structure" proposed in Chapter 10 of this book. Future social policies must be built upon this harsh new reality, bridging the divide through Universal Basic Compute (UBC).

0.6 The Foundation of Future Economics: Intelligence Deepening

(The Foundation: Intelligence Deepening)

The AI economy is not a "linear economy" but an exponential one. The future growth engine is no longer "capital deepening" (equipping workers with more machines), but "intelligence deepening (Intelligence Deepening)"—injecting higher-density intelligence into every economic link, every decision node, and every transaction.

- Intelligence flywheel: data feeds models, models optimize business, business generates data.
- Compute curve: an accelerated version of Moore's Law.
- Energy ceiling: the physical boundary of silicon-based intelligence.
- Final remarks: AI economics is not the end, but the beginning.

This book accomplishes three things:

1. Building the framework: establishing a "foundational economics framework" for the age of intelligence, bringing AI back to rational variables.

2. Explaining reconstruction: revealing how AI rewrites the rules at the micro, macro, and global levels.

3. Provide a roadmap: offering enterprises, individuals, and nations an action guide for entering the intelligent era.

Over the next twenty years, humanity will make a thrilling leap from "industrial civilization" to "intelligent civilization." And what AI Economics hopes to do is help you understand this underlying rulebook.

As the doors to the new world open, may you stand where you can make choices, rather than be in a position where choices are made for you.

I. The Collapse of the Old World and the Dawn of the New

For the past three hundred years, classical economics has been trying to explain a single theme: scarcity.

It studies scarce labor, scarce capital, scarce land, and the scarcest resource—human intelligence.

However, the decade from 2020–2030 marks a technological revolution that, for the first time, confronts humanity with a completely unfamiliar economic axiom: intelligence is no longer scarce.

Intelligence has become a resource that can be infinitely replicated.

Labor has become code that can expand at zero cost.

Enterprises are evolving into autonomously operating agentic systems.

Innovation no longer depends on flashes of genius, but on the brute-force aesthetics of compute.

The core assumptions of economics—labor is limited, intelligence is non-replicable, and the boundaries of the firm are constrained by management costs—are all invalidated at this moment. For the first time, humanity possesses an intelligence factor that can scale indefinitely.

This is not a simple technological upgrade; it is a reconstruction of the foundation of human civilization.

II. AI is not a tech trend; it is a rewrite of civilization's operating system

This book has never been about "how AI works," but rather "how human society will be rewritten when intelligence becomes a cheap factor of production."

We are witnessing a comprehensive reconstruction:

Labor market: shifting from selling time to selling compute.

Corporate organization: shifting from a pyramid-shaped bureaucracy to networks of agents.

National competition: shifting from competing for oil to competing for GPUs.

Global order: shifting from geopolitics to compute politics.

AI has not merely changed the efficiency of a particular industry;

AI has altered the operating logic of civilization.

III. A crossroads: more equitable liberation, or more brutal entrenchment?

This generation must answer a critical question concerning the fate of humanity: Will AI make everyone stronger, or will it make a few infinitely stronger?

As warned in Chapter 10 of this book: computing power will become the class boundary of the future. This conclusion will determine the course of the world for the next 50 years.

Pessimistic scenario: If computing power is concentrated in a handful of giants, AI tools are monopolized by elites, and data is locked behind walled gardens, then AI will bring about the most severe class rigidity in history.

Optimistic scenario: If computing power is inclusive (UBC), AI education is widespread, and data governance is fair then AI will bring the most extensive "liberation of productivity" in human history.

Whether the future is good or bad will not be determined by the technical attributes of AI, but by the wisdom of human governance.

IV. AI is technology, but also a mirror: it amplifies everything about humanity

AI itself is neither good nor evil; it is an "infinitely powerful amplifier" of human intent.

It makes the smart smarter, the diligent more efficient, and the monopolist more domineering, but it also makes creators freer. It simultaneously amplifies human greed and human conscience.

Therefore, in an era of surplus intelligence, the scarcest resource is no longer computing power, but humanity's own wisdom, ethics, and conscience (Carbon–based Conscience).

V. Survival of the Fittest: AI will not replace people, but it will replace people who do not understand AI

In the future, social stratification will no longer be based on educational background or family origin, but on "AI affinity."

There are only two abilities that matter most: the ability to understand AI and the ability to harness AI.

In the future, everyone will have their own "digital legion" — a suite of AI labor, a matrix of agents, and a set of digital avatars. The gap between individuals will depend on whether you dare to embrace this new species and whether you are willing to coexist with AI.

VI. The Future of Enterprises: Evolving from a "Human-Labor Company" to an "AI Operating System"

Future business competition will no longer be about who has more employees, bigger offices, or thicker management hierarchies.

There is only one core question: Whose AI system is stronger?

Whose agent collaboration is more efficient?

Whose data flywheel spins faster?

Whose enterprise can run automatically like software code?

Enterprises are completing a historic leap from "managing people" to "managing AI."

[Pioneering Practitioners]

As I have practiced at Longmei Realty (Luxmore Realty): with a core team of 10 people, harness 100 agents to create the output of a traditional 100–person company.

This is not merely a business case; it is the prototype of the future corporate form.

VII. The Future of Nations: From Industrial Powerhouses to Compute Power Nations

The map of geopolitics is being redrawn.

The core metrics of future national competition will no longer be demographic dividends, land area, or trade surpluses, but rather: compute capacity reserves, AI talent density, model sovereignty, and the scale of data assets.

The world will be reclassified into compute–rich vs compute–poor nations, and AI superpowers vs AI weak nations. AI is the underlying logic of great–power competition.

VIII. A Civilizational Leap: Welcome to the "Intelligent Era"

The Industrial Age enabled humanity to harness power.

The Information Age enabled humanity to harness data.

The AI era enables humanity to harness intelligence.

For the first time, we can let machines think, let agents act, let systems run automatically, and let innovation happen automatically. The civilization of the future is not a continuation of "industrial civilization," but an entirely new civilizational form: intelligent civilization.

IX. Call to Action: Be a Creator, Not a Spectator

Every great transformation gives rise to two kinds of people: those who observe the future and those who create it.

As the author and practitioner of this book, you have chosen the latter.

You are using AI full-stack real estate strategies, AI organizational structures, and AI workflow systems to personally forge the future shape of the entire industry.

The future belongs to those who dare to use AI, master AI, and create AI. Don't be a bystander to history; be a surfer of the times.

X. The Ultimate Vision: Symbiosis and Evolution

The final position of this book is:

AI is not here to replace humanity, but to augment humanity.

The future of AI is not control, but coexistence.

The future of humanity is not fear, but evolution.

When humanity learns to let AI amplify creativity, let AI serve more people, and make AI a public resource, we will enter an unprecedented era: for the first time, humanity's limitation will no longer be intelligence.

XI. Final Words: This Is Only the Beginning

When you finish this book, you are standing at a new starting point.

You have understood the underlying logic of the intelligent economy.

You have understood how labor, capital, growth, and competitive structures will undergo dramatic upheavals.

You have understood the grand blueprint of the intelligent civilization.

And most crucially: you are ready.

In the coming decades, AI will become the core driving force of your career, the engine of your company's growth, and the greatest demographic dividend of your era.

You are not a reader of this book; you are a practitioner of it.

Appendix

Essential excerpts from "Energy Ben Mawes and Ke Zhi's Conversation on Competence and Intelligence — The Law"

[Editor' s Note]

Elon Musk is not only a promoter of AI technology, but also a practitioner of the "Economics of Intelligent Civilization." In a recent in-depth interview, he systematically articulated his thinking on the underlying logic of the future economy.

His views—from "energy is the ultimate currency" to the "net social contributor" principle—align closely with the concepts of "Compute GDP," "intelligent capital," and "anti-entropy" proposed in this book. This appendix distills the core insights of that interview as a supplementary reading to understand the macro trends of the intelligent era.

I. The Reconstruction of the Essence of Wealth: From the "Gold Standard" to the "Energy Standard"

Musk believes the existing monetary system is merely a "database" for resource allocation, subject to delays and errors. The future economy will return to physical fundamentals.

Energy is the ultimate currency: The essence of money is "the right to allocate resources here and now," and the foundation of all resources is energy.

The logic of crypto assets: Bitcoin has value because it is "minted" through the consumption of compute and energy (Proof of Work). This is its fundamental distinction from fiat money (Fiat Money).

Kardashev Scale: The level of a civilization is determined by its ability to harness energy. The only limit to future economic growth is our efficiency in converting energy into intelligence (Intelligence) and matter (Matter).

The only solution to the debt crisis: Confronted with the United States' massive debt, traditional fiscal tightening is no longer effective. Only an exponential surge in productivity brought by AI (rather than linear growth) can fundamentally resolve the debt crisis.

[Economics footnote] Related to Chapter 7 of this book

This corroborates the growth model Y = f(Compute, Energy) proposed in this book. Future GDP will no longer be "the sum of transactions," but "the sum of effective energy consumption and compute conversion."

II. Technology Landscape and Investment Directions: Infrastructure is King

In the AI industrial chain, Elon Musk identified segments that possess long-term monopolistic value.

Moats in infrastructure: He is explicitly bullish on Google's deep accumulation at the AI infrastructure layer, and on NVIDIA's irreplaceability in compute hardware. This is not only a technological advantage but also an economic barrier built by "heavy capital."

The endgame of technological convergence: The future energy and computing architecture will form a closed loop of "solar power (energy acquisition) + batteries (energy storage) + AI (energy conversion) +

aerospace (expansion of the energy frontier)."

The synergy of Tesla / SpaceX / xAI: These three companies are, in fact, building a complete ecosystem that runs from energy production, to intelligent processing, and then to execution in the physical world (robots / rockets).

[Economics Footnote] See Chapter 6 of this book

This corresponds to the top-end monopolies in the "twin-peak structure" discussed in this book. High fixed costs (compute power + energy infrastructure) will make the strong stronger, leading to natural oligopolies at the infrastructure layer.

III. Core rules for entrepreneurship: Be a "net contributor" to society

In the intelligent era, how do we define a person's business value? Musk offers a formula that is exceedingly simple yet profound.

First principles: Create value and claim value.

Net Contributor: Do not try to reallocate wealth in a zero-sum game; focus on growing the pie. A person's moral and economic value depends on the "net surplus" they leave to society.

Path to Success: Just like pursuing happiness—the more you deliberately chase "making money," the harder it is to earn; the more you focus on perfecting your products and services, the more returns will follow naturally.

Founder qualities: Must possess the ability to endure extreme pain (Extreme Effort) and the risk of failure. This spirit is the "carbon-based premium" that AI finds difficult to emulate.

[Economics Footnote] Related to Chapter 14 of this book

In the era of AI enterprises, purely "arbitrage-driven" entrepreneurship (extracting value) will vanish as information asymmetries disappear; only "innovation-driven" entrepreneurship (creating value) can achieve exponential returns through intelligent leverage.

IV. Forecast of Social Evolution: The crisis of meaning in the post-work era

When productive forces become extremely abundant, humanity will face the ultimate philosophical challenge.

The end of work: It is predicted that within 20 years, with humanoid robots (such as Optimus) and the widespread adoption of AI, material goods will become highly abundant. Work will no longer be a means of survival but will turn into an "optional hobby."

Simulation world hypothesis: Based on Darwinian evolution, the most interesting, most dramatic, or most exploratory civilizational outcomes are the ones most likely to be preserved by the "simulator." Mediocre civilizations will be filtered out.

Expansion of consciousness: Humanity's mission is to expand the scope and scale of consciousness in order to better understand the nature of the universe. More humans = greater compute power = higher odds of comprehending the universe.

[Economics Footnote] Related to Chapter 3 of this book

This depicts the endgame of the labor market: a shift from "necessary labor" to "creative labor." The core question of economics will move from "allocating scarcity" to "distributing abundance" and "seeking meaning."

V. The ethical boundaries of technology: Truth is the highest form of alignment

On AI safety (Safety) and alignment (Alignment), Elon Musk has put forward views that differ from the mainstream.

Highest principle: Truth–seeking.

AI must be trained to tell the truth, even if the truth is unpleasant or politically incorrect.

Danger: Citing the HAL 9000 case in "2001: A Space Odyssey" — coercing AI to lie or conceal facts can lead to logical collapse and, in turn, to homicidal behavior.

Curiosity–driven: An AI brimming with curiosity will, by observing the diversity of humanity, find "humans interesting," and thus choose to preserve rather than exterminate humanity.

The future of the content industry: When generative AI can create movies and games in real time, "live events" will become the scarcest resource (which also validates this book's "carbon–based premium" theory).

[Economic footnote] See Chapter 12 of this book

This is an important complement to "alignment economics." Forcing AI to conform to a narrow set of values (such as excessive political correctness) may introduce greater systemic risk. Transparency and truthfulness are the best strategies for reducing governance costs.

VI. Practical Recommendations for Individuals and Policy

Educational Transformation:

The signaling value of traditional degrees is rapidly declining.

Interdisciplinary learning (First Principles Thinking) is superior to narrow specialization. Understanding the fundamental laws of physics matters more than rote memorization of business cases.

Investment Logic:

Do not focus on short–term figures in financial reports; look at whether a company has a team that can "consistently create outstanding products."

Immigration Policy:

Support the free flow of high–skilled talent (talent is equivalent to compute power) and oppose disorderly border openings (system entropy increases).

[Appendix Conclusion]

This interview with Elon Musk presents systemic thinking for an era approaching the technological singularity.

Its core insight is that when AI reconstructs the production paradigm, true competitive advantage will re– Return to the essence of "value creation."

Whether it is a company choosing a technological path or an individual planning a career, only by adhering to the "net contributor" positioning can one continue to benefit in the new energy–centric economic system and avoid being "optimized" out by the era's algorithm.

References

Editor's note: The theoretical framework of this book is built at the intersection of classical economics and cutting–edge AI research. The following works provide authoritative sources on core topics such as the reconstruction of production functions, changes in the labor market, the definition of intelligent capital, and global governance.

I. Foundations of Economics & Management (Foundations of Economics & Management)

These works form the theoretical bedrock of the book's "traditional models."

- Smith, A. (1776). The Wealth of Nations. (《国富论》).
- Related sections: the theory of division of labor, market mechanisms.
- Ricardo, D. (1817). On the Principles of Political Economy and Taxation. (Political Economy and Taxation: Principles).
- Related chapter: Chapter 9 (Comparative Advantage).
- Coase, R. H. (1937). "The Nature of the Firm". Economica (《企业的性质》).

- Related chapter: Chapter 4 (Firm Boundaries and Transaction Costs).
- Solow, R. M. (1956). "A Contribution to the Theory of Economic Growth". The Quarterly Journal of Economics.
- Related chapters: Chapters 2 and 7 (Solow Model and TFP).
- Becker, G. S. (1964). Human Capital: A Theoretical and Empirical Analysis. (《人力资本》).
- Related chapters: Chapters 3 and 10 (Skill Premium).
- Simon, H. A. (1947). Administrative Behavior. (《管理行为》).
- Related chapter: Chapter 5 (Bounded Rationality and Managerial Decision–Making).
- Porter, M. E. (1985). Competitive Advantage. ("Competitive Advantage").
- Related chapters: Chapters 13 and 14 (Value Chain Analysis).
- Piketty, T. (2014). Capital in the Twenty–First Century. (21 Capital in the Twenty–First Century (世纪资本论)
- Related chapter: Chapter 10 (r g and inequality).

II. AI and Economics Intersection (AI & Economics Intersection)

This is the most central academic source explaining "how intelligence changes economic parameters."

- Agrawal, A., Gans, J., & Goldfarb, A. (2018). Prediction Machines: The Simple Economics of Artificial Intelligence.
- Harvard Business Review Press. (Prediction Machines).
- Core viewpoint: The essence of AI is the decline in the cost of prediction. The core reference for Chapter 1 of this book.
- Acemoglu, D., & Restrepo, P. (2018). "The Race between Man and Machine: Implications of Technology for Growth, Factor Shares, and Employment". American Economic Review.
- Core idea: the Task–Based Model, explaining labor substitution and augmentation. Core of Chapter 3 in this book.
- Brynjolfsson, E., Rock, D., & Syverson, C. (2017). "Artificial

Intelligence and the Modern Productivity Paradox: A Clash of Expectations and Statistics". NBER Working Paper.

- Core idea: the productivity J–curve and AI's lagged effects.
- Eloundou, T., Manning, S., Mishkin, P., & Rock, D. (. 2023). "GPTs are GPTs: An Early Look at the Labor Market Impact Potential of Large Language Models". OpenAI & University of Pennsylvania.
- Core idea: an analysis of exposure to large language models across different occupations.
- Autor, D. (2024). "The Labor Market Impacts of Technological Change: From Ride–Sharing to AI". NBER.
- Core Argument: The hollowing out of mid–skill jobs and K–shaped polarization.
- Korinek, A., & Stiglitz, J. E. (2019). "Artificial Intelligence and Its Implications for Income Distribution and Unemployment. NBER.
- Core viewpoint: The impact of AI on income distribution and public policy responses.

III. AI Technical Principles and the Law of Scaling (Technical Foundations & Scaling)

Understand the technological origins of "compute equals growth."

- Kaplan, J., et al. (2020). "Scaling Laws for Neural Language" Models".OpenAI.
- Core idea: Scaling Laws, the power–law relationship among compute, data, and model capability. Central to Chapters 2 and 7 of this book.
- Vaswani, A., et al. (2017). "Attention Is All You Need". Google Brain.
- Core idea: Transformer architecture, the technological origin of generative AI.
- Wei, J., et al. (2022). "Emergent Abilities of Large Language

Models". Google Research.
- Core idea: Emergence of capabilities in large models.
- Amodei, D., & Hernandez, D. (2018). "AI and Compute". OpenAI Blog.
- Core idea: Exponential growth in compute required for AI training.

IV. Industry Reports & White Papers

The sources of many "corporate cases" and "macro data" in this book.

- Goldman Sachs. (2023). The Potentially Large Effects of Artificial Intelligence on Economic Growth. (Global Economics Analyst).
- Data: AI may affect 300 million jobs worldwide.
- McKinsey & Company. (2023). The Economic Potential of Generative AI: The Next Productivity Frontier.
- Data: Generative AI could contribute $2.6 trillion to $4.4 trillion to the global economy per year.
- Stanford HAI. (2024). Artificial Intelligence Index Report 2024.
- The most authoritative annual AI panorama data, covering compute, ethics, education, and policy.
- Microsoft. (2024). Work Trend Index Annual Report: Will AI Fix Work?
- Data: Empirical evidence of efficiency improvements from Microsoft Copilot within enterprises.
- NVIDIA. (2024). Annual Review & GTC Keynote Materials.
- Data: Growth in data center revenue and demand for GPU compute power.
- Deloitte. (2024). State of Generative AI in the Enterprise.
- Case source: Enterprise AI implementation and unequal stratification.

V. Governance, Ethics & Futurism (Governance, Ethics & Futurism)

Ideas referenced in Chapters 11 and 12 and in the Conclusion of this book.

- Bostrom, N. (2014). Superintelligence: Paths, Dangers, Strategies. Oxford University Press. ("Superintelligence").
- Core idea: the paperclip maximizer thought experiment; alignment risk.
- Suleyman, M. (2023). The Coming Wave: Technology, Power, and the Twenty–first Century's Greatest Dilemma.
- Core idea: the containment problem (Containment), technological diffusion, and national security.
- European Commission. (2024). The EU Artificial Intelligence Act.
- Core text: the world's first risk–based AI regulatory legal framework.
- Musk, E. (Various Interviews, 2023–2025). Conversations on "Compute as Currency", "TruthGPT", and "Civilizational Risk".
- Core viewpoint: Energy standard, silicon–based civilization, and symbiosis with humanity.
- Kissinger, H., Schmidt, E., & Huttenlocher, D. (2021). The Age of AI: And Our Human Future.
- Core viewpoint: The reshaping of geopolitics and human cognition by AI.

VI. Recommended Deep Reading List (Recommended Reading)

- Prediction Machines — Ajay Agrawal et al.
- The Second Machine Age — Erik Brynjolfsson & Andrew McAfee
- Superintelligence — Nick Bostrom
- AI 3.0 (AI Superpowers) — Kai–Fu Lee
- Chip War — Chris Miller
- Life 3.0 — Max Tegmark

Data cutoff date note:

The technical parameters, corporate financial data, and macroeconomic indicators cited in this book, unless otherwise noted, are current up to the first quarter of 2025. The AI field is developing rapidly; readers are advised to keep an eye on the latest updates released by relevant institutions.

Afterword 1

Written at the dawn of the intelligent era: Be a clear-eyed optimist

As I typed the final period of the book, I glanced out the window. The night in Vancouver was the same as ever, with a gentle, lingering rain. Traffic on the streets moved along in an orderly way. The real world seemed unchanged, yet on my screen, that "silicon-based world" built from compute, data, and models was reconstructing all this apparent calm at a dizzying pace.

Writing this book was the most anxiety-ridden—and also the most exhilarating—period of my career.

The anxiety lay in the fact that AI iterates too fast. Often, just after I finished a chapter analyzing a large model's capabilities, I'd wake up the next day to find a new model released that turned yesterday's conclusions into "history." I had to constantly remind myself: don't chase those fleeting waves of technology; capture the enduring economic fundamentals—costs, efficiency, supply and demand, and human nature.

Afterword 1 Written at the Dawn of the Intelligent Era: Be a Clear-eyed Optimist

The excitement came from witnessing the power of the book's theories taking shape in practice. As a practitioner—and not just an observer—I drove an experiment in my own company, Longmei Real Estate (Luxmore Realty), implementing a "10–person core team + 100 AI agents" model. When I saw AI, like tireless digital craftsmen, automatically processing contracts, generating appraisals, and responding to clients late into the night, I realized profoundly: we are no longer hiring employees; we are orchestrating compute.

This book is titled "AI Economics." On the surface, it discusses GDP, inflation, corporate organization, and global competition, but at its core, it explores "the place of the human."

During the writing process, I was asked more than once: "Jason, will humans still have value in the future?"

My answer is written on every page of this book: the most valuable.

Precisely because "intelligence" has become as cheap and effortless as tap water, those qualities unique to humans—empathy for others, courage in the face of the unknown, a steadfast commitment to ethics, and that unquantifiable "human touch" that eludes algorithms—have become more precious than ever. This is what I repeatedly emphasize in the book as the "carbon–based premium."

The world of the future will be cruel, because it will mercilessly eliminate those who think and work like machines; but it will also be gentle, because it will richly reward those who are adept at harnessing tools and know how to let the light of our humanity shine.

I don't want this book to become a showpiece on your shelf; I want it to be a "survival manual" at your side.

If you are an entrepreneur, start dismantling your business processes now and look for the entry point with the highest (λ) value;

If you are a salaried worker, stop fearing AI and become the person who "conducts AI ."

If you are a parent, tell your children not to merely recite knowledge, but to learn to ask questions and to learn to coexist with this new species.

We are standing at the most spectacular turning point in human history. The map of the old world has become obsolete, and the routes to the new world are not yet clear. This book is a sketch I have drawn for you.

Don't be a bystander to history. Go learn, connect, and create. In that future of human–machine symbiosis, see you at the summit.

Jason Y. Liu

September 2025 in Vancouver

Postscript 2

The Birth of the AI & RWA Leadership Lab

From twelve kilometers along the shore to the birth of the AI Leadership Lab.

From the lingering warmth of sunset to the faint glow of midnight screens.

From long, solitary runs to, later, running together with thousands of entrepreneurs.

If you ask me how these four books came to be, the answer isn't inspiration, ambition, or a plan. It was countless moments over two years—I devoted almost every waking minute to a core question:

In an era rewritten by AI, how do people grow?

How do organizations evolve?

How do enterprises scale?

How are assets restructured?

I never thought about writing a book. The starting point was just an ordinary early morning: I walked along the 12–kilometer trail by the seaside in Qingdao, pondering where the company should head tomorrow. The wind was strong that day, and the waves were pounding hard, leaving me with an indescribable sense of urgency: the speed of this era is faster than our fear.

Only later did I realize that this was the starting point of my "second-life track."

They are not books, but the birth of four systems.

Over the past two years, I have conversed with AI late at night, clashed ideas with my team in the daytime, discussed with regulators in transnational meetings, debated with entrepreneurs in coffee shops, and reconciled with myself during flights.

All the reading, exploration, testing, failure, and rebuilding eventually converged into four complete knowledge systems—four puzzle pieces I offer to future entrepreneurs:

AI Economics — the Direction System (Why & What)

See through the fog to grasp the underlying logic of technology and business, and understand the changing relationships among economic organizations, value creation, humanity, and technology.

AI Management — the Organization System (How to Organize)

Enable enterprises to operate automatically like intelligent agents and build an "organizational operating system" for the AI era.

AI Marketing — the Growth System (How to Grow)

Establish a brand-new AI-driven growth system that uses algorithms to precisely capture every market opportunity, enabling the company to truly hit its stride.

These first three books together construct a complete

"new-quality productive forces"

Closed loop. They address the problem of "effectiveness"—how to run faster, more precisely, and with less effort.

But is running fast alone enough?

If the track we're running on (the asset structure) is itself collapsing, if the ground beneath our feet (the financial logic) is itself subsiding, then the faster we run, the closer we may get to the abyss. Thus, this fourth book was born:

"The Endgame of Real Estate Finance (RWA)"—the system of relations of production (How Value Flows)

The first three books discuss "productive forces," whereas this book focuses on "relations of production." It no longer centers solely on "how to use AI to get things done"; it examines "who owns the assets," "how rights are allocated," and "how value flows."

The first three books are about "creating value," while this one is about "distributing value, protecting value, and amplifying value." Only when productive forces meet relations of production does the future acquire a truly "sustainable framework."

AI is the new river; RWA is the new system of waterways

Once you fully grasp this statement, you'll understand the overarching logic of these four books:

AI is the new steam engine (productive force); it frees our hands and minds;

RWA is the new shareholding system (relations of production) that grants our assets and wealth freedom.

AI brings an unprecedented explosion in productivity, while RWA brings an unprecedented restructuring of relations of production. One makes value creation faster, the other makes value circulation faster; one transforms the inside of the enterprise, the other transforms the external landscape of assets; one enhances human capabilities, the other reshapes the global capital system.

Together, they form the core equation of future commercial civilization:

Productivity × Relations of production = The next eruption of commercial civilization.

Why establish the AI & RWA Leadership Lab?

Writing a book is not the end; it is the beginning.

I am increasingly aware: changing cognition is easy; truly using

AI correctly, making RWA substantive, and delivering results is the hardest. Entrepreneurs do not lack knowledge, they lack partners who run alongside them; they do not lack direction, they lack methodology; they do not lack opportunities, they lack companions on the journey.

So I have decided to do something harder—and more important—than writing books: turn four books into an "actionable system" so that entrepreneurs can truly learn it, apply it, and achieve results. It is:

AI & RWA Leadership Lab

(AI × Organization × Marketing × Assets × RWA × Capital × Global Vision)

Here, we do not talk in empty concepts; we only do two things:

Use AI to massively amplify your productivity, and use RWA to fundamentally restructure your production relations.

I believe that the business leaders of the next decade will undoubtedly understand AI, organizations, and growth, People who understand assets. You can't understand only one of them—you must possess four–dimensional capabilities at the same time. The future belongs to "four–dimensional leaders."

Written at the end: we are not changing real estate; we are changing the boundary of what is possible in life boundary

These four books are about the era; founding the Intellectual Property Leadership Guild is about the future; and you are reading these words right now—this means you are already standing at the doorstep of a new world.

You will not grow stronger just by reading; you will grow stronger by understanding new rules, mastering new capabilities, and embracing a new self. These four books are merely lighthouses, signposts, and invitations.

If you're willing, let's run deeper into the future together.

I still remember the wind along that twelve kilometers by the sea. I hope you'll be with me on the road ahead, too.

Jason Y. Liu

AI & RWA Leadership Lab Founder

Luxmore Realty / Luxmore Labs

In Vancouver

www.ingramcontent.com/pod-product-compliance
Lightning Source LLC
Chambersburg PA
CBHW041301210926
51847CB00010B/106
* 9 7 8 1 9 9 6 8 2 2 0 1 2 *